Bible Messages

by

Oliver B. Greene

The Gospel Hour, Inc., Oliver B. Greene, Director
Box 2024, Greenville, South Carolina   29602

FOREWORD

The messages in this book were originally printed in booklet form, and the Lord has graciously used them to bless the hearts of many people. As they go forth in this new form, it is my sincere prayer that He will use them in an even greater way, and that His name will receive all honor and praise for whatever may be accomplished through them.

The Author

CONTENTS

CONTENTS

Where Are the Dead?

WHERE ARE THE DEAD?

My home is just across the road from a cemetery, and daily I hear the funeral chimes send out the haunting, mellow notes of "God Be With You Till We Meet Again." More than once I have wiped tears from my eyes as I listened to that sweet music; and as it played, I have seen a weeping mother leave the grave of her child, or a heartbroken wife walk away from the grave of her beloved husband. I have heard the clear, golden notes of those chimes a thousand times in the last few years — but I have never grown accustomed to them. Each time I hear them they remind me of one Christmas Day when I placed my own little boy in the grave, and I remember how empty everything seemed without him.

DEATH! What a mysterious thing death is! The Bible tells us, "It is appointed unto men once to die" (Heb. 9:27) and graveyards give silent but undeniable testimony to the truth of that Scripture. I repeat — What a mysterious thing death is.

What happens when dad or mother, baby or grandmother, leaves this world in death? There are so many ideas about the dead. Religions have done a wonderful job of confusing people on the subject. Men have formed opinions, and have subsequently twisted the Word of God to fit their own ideas and doctrines. But beloved, in this study *we will use the word of God as it is;* we will neither add to nor take from the plain truth concerning the dead — where they are and what they are doing.

Who is responsible for death? Is God the author of it? Romans 5:12 answers: "Wherefore, *as by one man* sin entered into the world, and *death by sin;* and so death passed upon all men, for that all have sinned."

9

When Adam disobeyed God and ate of the forbidden fruit (Gen. 2:17) he died; and through his disobedience, death moved upon all men. In Adam all die — but thank God, in Christ all can be made alive! The first Adam is the author of death; the second Adam (the Lord Jesus Christ) is the author of life. Jesus said ". . . He that believeth in me, though he were dead, yet shall he live: And whosoever liveth and believeth in me shall never die" (John 11:25, 26 in part).

Man is the author of death; *God* is the author of life. I Corinthians 15:26 tells us, *"The last enemy that shall be destroyed is death."* Had Adam not eaten of the tree of the knowledge of good and evil, man would never have died: ". . . . The Lord God said, Behold, the man is become as one of us, to know good and evil: and now, lest he put forth his hand, and *take also of the tree of life, and eat, and live forever:* Therefore the Lord God sent him forth from the garden of Eden . . . and He placed at the east of the garden of Eden Cherubim and a flaming sword which turned every way, to keep the way of the tree of life" (Gen. 3:22-24 in part).

What happens when a person dies? What takes place when the eyelids close, the lips become silent, and the body lies motionless in death? All who are not atheists admit that Jesus died on the cross. Where did He go when He died? The only place to find the right answer is in the Word of God:

On the morning of the resurrection, Mary went to the tomb of Jesus and found it empty. The angels who were in attendance asked her why she wept, and she said, "Because they have taken away my Lord, and I know not where they have laid Him." She saw Jesus standing by, but she failed to recognize Him. Supposing Him to be the gardner she said to Him, "Sir, if thou have borne Him (Jesus) hence, tell

10

me where thou hast laid Him, and I will take Him away. Jesus said unto her, Mary. She turned herself, and saith unto Him, Rabboni; which is to say, Master. Jesus saith unto her, Touch me not; for I am not yet ascended to my Father" (John 20-11-17).

At this time, Jesus had been dead for three days; where had He been? Had He been unconscious? Had He been asleep? If Jesus lay unconscious or asleep in the grave, then the Bible is a lie; but we know the Bible is NOT a lie: *It is the truth of God.*

In Matthew 12:38-40, the Pharisees asked Jesus for a sign. He replied, ". . . There shall no sign be given . . . but the sign of the prophet Jonas: For as Jonas was three days and three nights in the whale's belly; so shall the Son of man be three days and three nights *in the heart of the earth.*"

One need not have a diploma from college to know where the heart of the earth is. The heart of the earth certainly is not in Jerusalem in Joseph's tomb where the body of Jesus was laid when they took Him down from the cross. The heart of the earth is the center of this globe on which we live, and science knows the center of this earth to be a mass of liquid, molten fire. In some places, boiling water comes forth from the ground; in other places, mountains belch forth melted rock and fire. (We call these eruptions "volcanoes.") The Scripture tells us that when Jesus died, He went to the heart of the earth.

At that time, Paradise was located in the heart of the earth, and the souls of the saints who had died from Adam to Calvary went to that Paradise. Jesus spent three days in the heart of the earth, just as He said He would do. In Ephesians 4:8-10 Paul plainly tells us, "Wherefore He saith, When He ascended up on high, *He led captivity captive,* and gave gifts unto men. (Now that He ascended,

11

what is it but that He also descended first into the lower parts of the earth? He that descended is the same also that ascended up far above all heavens, that He might fill all things.)" Please read Isaiah 61:1 and Luke 4:18 in connection with this. Jesus came to earth to die for the sins of the world; but in so doing He purchased deliverance for the captives resting in the Paradise side of hell — which was then located in the lower parts of this earth.

We know that Jesus is the resurrection and the life (John 11:25, 26). According to the inspired words of the Apostle Paul, to be absent from the body is to be present with the Lord. Zechariah spoke of the Old Testament saints as "prisoners of hope" (Zech. 9:12). And at the close of the great roll call of the faithful in Hebrews 11:39, 40 Paul says, "And these all, having obtained a good report through faith, *received not the promise:* God having provided some better thing for us, that they without us should not be made perfect." Since the resurrection of the Lord Jesus, the spirits of believers at death go to the Paradise above. The Paradise in the heart of the earth has been incorporated into the hell of fire (Isa. 5:14).

"For thou wilt not leave my soul in hell; neither wilt thou suffer thine Holy One to see corruption" (Psalm 16:10). These same words are found in Acts 2:27, and they refer to none other than the Lord Jesus. Jesus did go to the Paradise side of hell — not the torment side; and He stayed there three days and nights. When He came out, He brought with Him every saint who had died since Adam. Many of them walked the streets of Jerusalem: ". . . And the earth did quake, and the rocks rent; and the graves were opened, and many BODIES of the saints which slept arose, *and came out of the graves after His resurrection, and went into the holy city, and appeared unto many"* (Matt. 27:52, 53).

Please note: "The *bodies* of the saints arose," The body

12

is the tabernacle, the house, from which the saints had moved at death. Had Jesus taught soul-sleep He would have said, "Many of the *sleeping saints* arose," but the Scripture says the BODIES of the saints arose.

Jesus was the God-Man: He was GOD — yet He was MAN. He took upon Himself "the likeness of sinful flesh, and for sin, condemned sin in the flesh." He was a man just as we are men, but He was infinitely more: He was the God-Man. In Hebrews 2:14 Paul says, "Forasmuch then as the children are partakers of flesh and blood, *He also Himself likewise took part of the same,* that through death He might destroy him that had the power of death, that is, the devil." Jesus took the *flesh part* of man. He tasted life in every respect just as we do; and furthermore, He tasted death for us, and by so doing removed the sting of death for believers.

"But we see Jesus, who was made a little lower than the angels for the suffering of death, crowned with glory and honour; that He by the grace of God should taste death for every man" (Heb. 2:9).

"O death, where is thy sting? O grave, where is thy victory? The sting of death is sin; and the strength of sin is the law. But thanks be to God, which giveth us the victory through our Lord Jesus Christ" (I Cor. 15:55-57).

"For what the law could not do, in that it was weak through the flesh, God sending His own Son in the likeness of sinful flesh, and for sin, condemned sin in the flesh: That the righteousness of the law might be fulfilled in us, who walk not after the flesh, but after the Spirit" (Rom. 8:3, 4).

"Forasmuch then as the children are partakers of flesh and blood, He also Himself likewise took part of the same; that through death He might destroy him that had the power of death, that is, the devil; *and deliver them who through fear of death were all their lifetime subject to bondage.* For verily He took not on Him the nature of angels; but He took on Him the seed of Abraham" (Heb. 2:14-16).

These Scriptures outline exactly what Jesus came into the world to do, and what He DID do by His coming: *Because* Jesus died and rose again, the *taste of death* has been removed for believers, the *sting of death* has been removed, the *fear of death* has been removed, and thank God, BONDAGE has been replaced WITH PERFECT LIBERTY! Now we are ready to discuss what happens when a believer takes that last breath and the doctors pronounce him dead:

"For we *know* that if our earthly house (body) of this tabernacle were dissolved, we have a building of God, *an house not made with hands,* eternal in the heavens" (II Cor. 5:1). This verse refers to our earthly house, our body. "For in this we groan, earnestly desiring to be clothed upon *with our house which is from heaven*" (II Cor. 5:2). That verse speaks of our glorified bodies which we will have when Jesus comes again: ". . . We know that, when He shall appear, *we shall be like Him:* for we shall see Him as He is" (I John 3:2).

"For we that are in this tabernacle do groan, being burdened: not for that we would be unclothed, but clothed upon, that mortality might be swallowed up of life . . . Therefore we are always confident knowing that, whilst we (the soul) are at home in the body (the house we live in), we are absent from the Lord . . . We are confident, I say, and willing rather to be *absent from the body,* and to be *present with the Lord*" (II Cor. 5:4, 6, 8).

That passage of Scripture clearly teaches that the spirit of the believer goes to be with the Lord the moment the last breath leaves the body. The spirit is not absent from the body in sleep or unconsciousness somewhere until Jesus

14

comes or until the resurrection of the body; the BODY goes to sleep, but the SPIRIT returns to God.

"In the sweat of thy face shalt thou eat bread, till thou return unto the ground; for out of it wast thou taken: for dust thou art, and unto dust shalt thou return" (Gen. 3:19). You may ask, "Does that not teach that man goes back to dust?" The answer to that question is found in Genesis 2:7: "And the Lord God formed man of the dust of the ground, and BREATHED INTO HIS NOSTRILS THE BREATH OF LIFE; and man became a living soul!"

Yes, man was formed of dust — but he became a living soul when God breathed into him the breath of life. In Genesis 1:20-23 when the animals were created, not one word is said about God breathing life into these living creatures. That is the difference between man and the lower order of animals. Animals have a *created life,* and that life ceases at death; but not so with *man's* life. *Man's life is God-breathed:* "Then shall the dust return to the earth as it was: and the spirit shall return unto God who gave it" (Eccl. 12:7).

Those who teach the false doctrine of soul-sleep and the unconsciousness of the dead do not separate body, soul, and spirit. They teach that the body is *you,* and that *when that body stops breathing, you stop existing* until the resurrection. But that is not what the Bible teaches. In this message we will just listen to the plain Word of God, for it is there that we will find the truth about life after death.

The Word speaks in plain, understandable language: "For me to live is Christ, and *to die is gain.* But if I (my spirit) live in the flesh (my body) this is the fruit of my labour: yet what I shall choose I wot not. For I am in a strait betwixt two, having a desire to *depart, and to be with Christ;* which is far better: Nevertheless to *abide in the flesh* is more needful for you" (Phil. 1:21-24).

Paul did not believe that his flesh was himself. He said that he *lived* in the flesh, but he did not teach that his flesh was more than the house in which he lived. Paul said, "To die is gain." Could one sleeping unconscious in a grave be said to have *gained* in dying? Please note that in these verses Paul makes plain the fact that he had a desire to *depart and be with Christ* — not to depart and be left sleeping in a grave! Paul said he had a desire to be where Jesus is. To teach that Paul is now sleeping, that he has been unconscious in a grave since his death, is to teach that *Jesus* is unconscious and still asleep in the tomb!

Philippians is one of the prison letters. Paul was in prison for preaching the Gospel of the marvelous grace of God, and the dear old apostle desired to go on home to be with the Lord; but he knew that the saints at Philippi needed him, and he was never a shirker of his duty. Therefore he said, "To abide (live) in the flesh (in my body) is more needful for you." Had Paul been called upon to seal his testimony with his life's blood that every day, he knew that he would immediately go to be with the Lord — which would be far better for him than remaining in the Philippian jail.

Peter believed and preached just as Paul did. He acknowledged that the tabernacle (body) in which he lived was not really himself, that the flesh is simply the house in which the real man lives. He spoke of his body as soon to be "put off," and made it plain that he believed what he said because the Lord showed it to him:

"Yea, I think it meet, *as long as I am in this tabernacle*, to stir you up by putting you in remembrance; knowing that shortly I must put off this, my tabernacle (body), *even as our Lord Jesus Christ hath shewed me*" (II Peter 1:13, 14).

I will take my stand with Peter, Paul, and every other writer of the New Testament. I thank God that I have everlasting life RIGHT NOW — not simply life that will last until death and at which time I will go into a state of unconsciousness and soul-sleep until the resurrection when the Lord Jesus will start my eternal life again. Oh, no! *I HAVE EVERLASTING LIFE NOW.* I am NOW living eternally! According to the Scriptures we have just studied, I will live in this body until I die, and when I die *my body* will return to dust (Gen. 2:9) but *my spirit will go to be with the Lord!* I will rest in Paradise with the other saints who have died since Calvary (Rev. 14:13) and when Jesus comes in the Rapture I will receive a glorified body like unto HIS glorious body. Amen!

The dear people who teach soul-sleep and an unconscious state of the dead take great joy in pointing out John 3:13: "No man hath ascended up to heaven, but He that came down from heaven, even the Son of man which is in heaven."

However, that verse is not hard to understand if we compare Scripture with Scripture, forgetting religions and doctrines of men. Nicodemus could not understand how he could be born when he was old; he asked Jesus, "How can these things be?" Jesus used the wind as an illustration, and then explained to Nicodemus that these things are taken by faith; by believing the Word of God, by believing what He (Jesus) was saying — and not by reasoning out the new birth from the standpoint of man's wisdom.

"Now this I say, brethren, that flesh and blood cannot inherit the kingdom of God; neither doth corruption inherit incorruption" (I Cor. 15:50). It is not the flesh and blood which go to heaven; it is the spirit and soul that go to Paradise at death.

". . . Enoch walked with God: and he was not; *for God took him*" (Gen. 5:24).

"And it came to pass, as they still went on, and talked, that, behold, there appeared a chariot of fire, and horses of fire, and parted them both asunder; *and Elijah went up*

17

by a whirlwind into heaven" (II Kings 2:11).

Is the language of these verses hard to understand? Must we call in someone who has been in a trance or who has had a revelation from another world to explain those simple words? The Word of God tells us that Elijah went to heaven in a chariot of fire, and I see no reason why I should doubt that plain statement. James 5:17 tells us that Elijah was a man of like passions as we are, and that means that he was just an ordinary fellow of flesh and blood. God used him — and when Elijah had finished the work God gave him to do, God took him to heaven in a chariot of fire. What happened to the body of Elijah? I do not know — nor am I concerned about it. What I DO know (and in which fact I rejoice) is the Bible truth of what happened to his spirit — *the real Elijah.* Did he go to sleep? Did God put him into a state of unconsciousness when He took him up in the chariot of fire? According to Matthew 17:1-3 such was not the case:

"And after six days Jesus taketh Peter, James, and John his brother, and bringeth them up into an high mountain apart, and was transfigured before them: and His face did shine as the sun, and His raiment was white as the light. And, behold, there appeared unto them *Moses and Elias talking with Him!"*

In the verse that follows, Peter called these two men by name, which is evidence that he clearly recognized them. Elijah was caught up to heaven 750 years before this meeting took place on the Mount of Transfiguration; yet he was very much alive and recognizable there on the mountaintop when he appeared with Moses, who had also been dead for hundreds of years. Those who teach soul-sleep say that this is only a parable and that the disciples were in a trance. It is sad to think that one who claims to be a Bible student would make such a statement about the transfiguration of

18

Jesus, for that passage is a reality just as surely as the virgin birth and Calvary are realities.

"And in the sixth month the angel Gabriel was sent from God unto a city of Galilee, named Nazareth, to a virgin espoused to a man whose name was Joseph, of the house of David; and the virgin's name was Mary. . . . And the angel said unto her, Fear not, Mary: for thou hast found favour with God. And, behold, thou shalt conceive in thy womb, and bring forth a son, and shalt call His name Jesus" (Luke 1:26 ff).

Is this account of the virgin birth a real, live story? Did it really happen as Gabriel said it would? If this passage is a reality, so also is Matthew 17 with its account of the transfiguration, and it is nothing short of willing ignorance to spiritualize or make a parable of that passage. Moses and Elijah were alive that day on the mountaintop, and they are alive today in Paradise—as is every other saint who has passed beyond this life.

David believed in immortality of the soul. The sad story of David's sin and the death of his baby is told in II Samuel chapters 11 and 12. In II Samuel 12:23 David said, "But now is he dead, wherefore should I fast? Can I bring him back again? I shall go to him, but he shall not return to me. In other words, David said, "My baby is dead, he has gone to another world. I cannot bring him back, but I shall go where he has gone." You may rest assured that David was not referring to the grave nor to unconsciousness. If David had believed in soul-sleep he would have said, "My baby is sleeping now, he is resting; and one day I, too shall go to sleep." But David knew his little boy had gone to be with the Lord—and thank God, I know that *our little boy* who left us when he was only two days old has also gone to this same place of peace and rest. Our little son is not sleeping in a graveyard—*he is where Jesus is!*

19

Those who teach soul-sleep remind us again and again that the Bible refers to the saints falling asleep. Yes, the Bible tells us that Stephen saw heaven opened, saw the glory of God, and Jesus standing on the right hand of God. As the mob stoned him to death, he prayed "Lord, lay not this sin to their charge. And when he had said this, *he fell asleep*" (Acts 7:54-60).

The passage in I Thessalonians 4:13-14 will clear up the question of Stephen and all other saints who are said to have fallen asleep: "But I would not have you to be ignorant, brethren, *concerning them which are asleep*, that ye sorrow not, even as others which have no hope. For if we believe that Jesus died and rose again, even so them also which *sleep in Jesus will God bring with Him.*"

Let us look at these verses in the light of God's complete, infallible Word, and pray for God to give us wisdom to understand them: Those who sleep are said to be *asleep in Jesus*—but where is JESUS? If he is in the grave, then those who sleep in Him are also in the grave with Him. But if Jesus is not in the grave, then those who sleep in Jesus are not in the grave. I repeat the question: *Where is Jesus?* Hebrews 1:3 answers: "Who . . . when He had by Himself purged our sins, *sat down on the right hand of the Majesty on high!*" According to the Word of God, Jesus is now at the right hand of God. (Read also I Timothy 2:5.) Since Jesus is at the right hand of God, and since the sleeping ones are "asleep in Jesus," then they, too, are in the Paradise of God where Jesus is!

"For this we say unto you by the word of the Lord, that we which are alive and remain unto the coming of the Lord shall not prevent (hinder) them which are asleep. For the Lord Himself shall descend from heaven with a shout, with the voice of the archangel, and with the trump of God: and the dead in Christ shall rise first: Then we which are alive and remain shall be caught up together with them in the clouds, to meet the Lord in the air: and so shall we ever be with the Lord" (I Thess. 4:15-17).

We know, then, that the Lord Jesus is not in a grave. He is at the right hand of God, and in due time He will descend from heaven with a shout! Please notice: This passage tells us that Christ will bring "the dead in Christ" WITH HIM when He comes. If the dead in Christ were sleeping in the grave, and yet Jesus is to descend from heaven, how shall He then bring with Him the sleeping ones? "The dead in Christ shall rise first" must then of necessity refer to bodies, and not to souls or spirits.

You see, beloved, the doctrine of soul-sleep simply will not stand up under the searching of the light of the rightly-divided Word. The soul and spirit of the righteous sleep in Jesus now, just as Lazarus rested in Abraham's bosom in Paradise. If Jesus were unconscious and asleep, so also are His saints; but if Jesus is alive and conscious, so also are those who die in Him. God's Holy Spirit gave us that passage because He did not want us to be ignorant concerning our departed loved ones—yet some dear people read those verses and refuse to believe them!

"Wherefore comfort one another with these words" (I Thess. 4:18). What comfort could it possibly be to me to know that my little boy and my father are sleeping in a graveyard? I say, NONE! But thank God, *it is a great comfort to me to know that my dad and my little son are both resting with Jesus* where Jesus is right now! I praise God for I Thessalonians 4:13-18!

Of what comfort could it be to all the precious mothers and wives who lost sons and husbands in the terrible wars of recent years to know that their precious loved ones are sleeping out there in the bottom of the ocean or in the jungle where their planes were shot down and wild animals de-

21

voured them as soon as their parachutes hit the ground? What comfort could it be to those who remain, to know that a dear son, husband, or brother lies buried yonder in an unmarked grave in a foreign land? There are thousands upon thousands of mothers, wives, sweethearts and sisters who have no idea what became of the bodies of their loved ones! *"Missing in action"* is all they heard. But if those boys were saved, their loved ones know that they are resting in Paradise with Jesus, awaiting the resurrection of the body in that great day when Jesus comes from heaven to redeem all creation. Jude 14 tells us that Jesus will come with tens of thousands of His saints. How can that be possible if those saints are sleeping in a grave in a cemetery?

Revelation 6:9-10 clearly teaches that there is a difference between body and soul: "And when he had opened the fifth seal, I saw under the altar *the souls of them* that were slain for the word of God, and for the testimony which they held: *And they cried with a loud voice . . ."* Please note that John saw *souls*, not *bodies*. He saw the souls of those who were martyred for the sake of the Gospel—and these souls *cried with a loud voice!*

Now let us consider that much-disputed passage in Luke 16:19-31 — so often called "The parable of Lazarus and Dives." But beloved, if that is a parable, then the virgin birth and Calvary are also parables! The story of Lazarus and the rich man is true—as true as the virgin birth and the blood atonement.

We know that Jesus often taught in parables, but where passages embrace such teaching, that passage clearly states that it is a parable, or that is it *"like unto . . ."* Some of the parables Jesus used are set forth in Matthew and repeated in Mark and Luke. We know the only way to rightly divide the Word of truth is to compare Scripture with Scripture, spiritual things with spiritual. ". . . The natural man receiveth not the things of the Spirit of God: for they are foolishness unto him: neither can he know them, because they are spiritually discerned" (I Cor. 2:14). Now let us turn to the first parable in the New Testament:

Matthew 13:1 ff: "The same day went Jesus out of the house, and sat by the seaside. And great multitudes were gathered together unto Him, so that He went into a ship, and sat; and the whole multitude stood on the shore. And He spake many things unto them in parables. . . ."

"Hear ye therefore the parable of the sower"—v. 18.

"Another parable put He forth"—v. 24.

"Another parable put He forth"—v. 31.

"Another parable spake He unto them"—v. 33.

"Declare unto us the parable"—vs. 36.

"Again, the kingdom of heaven is LIKE UNTO"—v. 44.

"Again, the kingdom of heaven is LIKE unto"—v. 45.

"Again, the kingdom is like unto"—v. 47.

"And Jesus answered and spake unto them again by parables, and said. . . ." (Matthew 22:1 ff).

"Now learn a parable of the fig tree"—Matthew 24:32.

"For the kingdom of heaven IS AS a man"—Matthew 25:14.

"And He spake a parable unto them, saying, The ground of a certain rich man brought forth plentifully"—Luke 12:16.

"He spake also this parable"—Luke 13:6.

"And He put forth a parable"—Luke 14:7.

"And He spake this parable unto them, saying" —Luke 15:3.

But now let us consider the passage previously mentioned, on Lazarus and Dives:

"THERE WAS A CERTAIN RICH MAN, which was clothed in purple and fine linen, and fared sumptuously every day" (Luke 16:19). Beloved, there is no more positive

statement in the entire Bible than that statement! *"There was"* tells us that the man WAS—he literally existed. The Word of God does not say, *"Suppose there was* a certain man clothed in fine linen etc . . ."* The Scripture plainly says, "There WAS a CERTAIN rich man." There were many wealthy men in that land, but this one was a *certain* rich man—a certain man who wore purple and fine linen and fared sumptuously every day. He was evidently fanatical about his riches.

Suppose in my sermon one day I said to my audience, "There was a certain rich man in Greenville, South Carolina who wore purple and fine linen all the time, lived like a king every day—and then one day he dropped dead and I am sure that he went to hell." Suppose you then asked me, "Brother Greene, *where* in Greenville did that man live? I believe I know him. What was his name?" And *then suppose* that I should answer you by saying, "Oh, no such fellow ever really lived in Greenville—I was only using that as an illustration!" *What would you think of me?* If I had told you in the outset that I was using the story *as an illustration,* you would not have entertained the idea that such a man ever lived in my home town; but if I made the statement that such a person DID live there, and had described in detail how he lived, and how he dressed—and had then told you that I was merely telling the story to illustrate a point, you would have a perfect right to call me a liar!

But notice verse 20 in this same passage: "And there was *a certain* beggar *named Lazarus.*" To be sure, there were many beggars in Jerusalem, but the one who lay at the gate of that "certain rich man" was named *Lazarus.* In Acts 9:10 we read, "And there was *a certain disciple* at Damascus, *named Ananias . . .*" Do you believe Ananias was a real man? Do you believe that he was really in Damascus? Do you believe the Holy Ghost spoke to him and told

24

him about Saul, who was then at Simon's house, praying? Is the story in Acts 9 a parable? If we do not accept the account of "the certain disciple named Ananias" as real, then we cannot accept the conversion of Saul of Tarsus! There are many other such comparisons in the Bible: "There was a certain man named Simon . . ."

"There was a certain man named Ananias, and his wife, Sapphira . . ." But we are most interested in the fact that *"there was a certain beggar named Lazarus."* Beloved, reverently and in the fear of God, knowing that I must face this statement at the judgment seat of Christ, I say that if Simon was real, if Ananias was real, if Saul of Tarsus was really converted as the Scripture records it, then *Lazarus was a real, live man who laid at the rich man's gate,* and God has spoken through the Holy Ghost in order to help us to know the terribleness of hell!

The Bible tells me that there was *a certain rich man,* and that a certain *beggar named Lazarus,* lay, full of sores, at that rich man's gate and begged for crumbs that fell from the rich man's table. I believe the record just as it is written, and I expect to meet Lazarus when I get to Paradise!

Verse 22: "And it came to pass, that the beggar died, and was carried by the angels into Abraham's bosom . . ."

Those who believe in soul-sleep want an explanation of how Lazarus could get into the bosom of Abraham. To understand that statement we must turn to other Scripture which sheds light on what is meant by *"in the bosom of Abraham."*

John 1:18: "No man hath seen God at any time; the only begotten Son, which is in the bosom of the Father, He hath declared Him." At the time John spoke those words, Jesus was here on earth ready to begin His public ministry. That statement simply means that Jesus abode with the Father, *in the home* with the Father, in the *resting place* with the

25

Father.

Abraham is the father of the faithful. In Genesis 12:1-3 God called him out of his native land, "and Abraham went out, not knowing whither he went." In John 8:33 the Pharisees said, "We be Abraham's seed," and *spiritually* speaking, *we* are Abraham's seed. Abraham is the father of the faithful, and *Abraham's bosom is the resting place of the faithful!* "Bosom" indicates rest—a baby rests upon the bosom of its mother. What Luke 16:22 points out is that the poor, miserable beggar who asked for crumbs from the rich man's table *went to rest* the moment he died, and he is now with Abraham, the father of the faithful.

Those who teach soul-sleep teach that the entire man goes to the grave when he dies—that is, if man has a body, a soul, and a spirit, they go down into Sheol and remain there, unconscious, until the resurrection. To them, Abraham's bosom is the grave. To save my life I cannot understand how any person can be so blind! Why did not the Holy Spirit simply say, "And it came to pass that the beggar died and was carried by the angels *into the grave and peacefully put to sleep until the resurrection"?* If that was what God meant to tell us, then why did not the Holy Spirit make it plain?

HE DID MAKE IT PLAIN: "And it came to pass, that the beggar died, and *was carried by the angels into Abraham's bosom*: The rich man also died, and *was buried.*" Personally, I do not believe Lazarus was ever put into a grave. Had he been buried, the Bible would have said so. In all probability, his dead body was collected from the street by garbage men and thrown into the garbage dump. But that did not matter because the moment Lazarus drew his last breath his spirit took flight to Paradise—the resting place of the righteous.

26

The rich man *was buried*—no doubt his funeral was one of pomp and great dignity, as befitting his station in this life. BUT—"IN HELL HE LIFTED UP HIS EYES, being in torments, and seeth Abraham afar off, and Lazarus in his bosom" (Luke 16:23). Verse 24 of this chapter records the beginning of a conversation which could only be carried on by a man who had the ability to reason. He had the sensitivity of feeling; and he had all five senses which he had possessed in this life.

He opened his eyes—*and recognized Lazarus in Paradise.*

He opened his mouth—*and cried to Abraham.*

He knew what water was, what it was for, and he craved one drop of it to cool his parching tongue.

He had feelings—he said, "I am tormented in this flame!"

He knew what was tormenting him—he knew it was a flame, *fire.*

He remembered his father's house, and the fact that he had five brothers.

He asked that Lazarus be sent to his brothers to tell them not to come to the place of torment in which he found himself. Common sense tells us that the rich man was not in a grave, desiring that his brothers not come to join him there, for *every person must go to the grave* except those who live until Jesus comes. The rich man did not want Lazarus to go and warn his five brothers not to come to the grave—he wanted that dear beggar to return to earth and tell his brothers not to come to HELL—a hell of flame in which he was then suffering!

The rich man said, "If one went unto them *from the dead,* they will repent." He believed that it would be possible for one to return to this earth bodily—yes, even after that one had died with rotten leprosy.

Abraham reminded him that his brothers had Moses and

27

the prophets—that is, they had the Word of God (the books of Moses and the prophets) and if they would not believe the Word, neither would they believe even though one returned from the dead and warned them.

"But Abraham said, Son, remember that thou in thy lifetime receivedst thy good things, and likewise Lazarus evil things: *but now he is comforted, and thou art tormented.*" Note the use of present tense: ". . . He IS comforted . . . thou ART tormented." The beggar is comforted NOW; the rich man is tormented NOW. There is no way around that simple, plain statement of Scripture except for those who desire to make the Bible say what they *want* it to say, who twist the Word of God to fit their religion, instead of fitting their religion into the Word of God.

Luke 16:19-31 plainly teaches that the righteous go to Paradise the moment they die physically, and it also teaches that the wicked go immediately to hell where there is a flame of fire which torments them day and night. No fundamental Bible teacher will tell you that this passage from Luke is a parable. Only those who follow false cults and "isms," who desire to prove their point of soul-sleep would dare claim such. Those who rightly divide the Word know that this is no parable.

Where is Paradise? Does the Bible tell us? Can the location of Paradise be scripturally proved? Jesus said to the thief on the cross, "TODAY shalt thou be with me in Paradise" (Luke 23:43). Where did Jesus go that day? He died, and the thief also died—and *that very day* Jesus and the saved thief went to the heart of this earth into Abraham's bosom—the Paradise of the righteous in the Old Testament era. Read carefully Matthew 12:40 and Ephesians 4:7-10. Jesus remained in the heart of the earth for a period of three days and three nights; then He arose from the dead—bodily. He brought the captives out of Paradise in the cen-

28

ter of the earth and carried them to Paradise above—the same Paradise of which Paul testifies in II Corinthians 12:1-4:

"It is not expedient for me doubtless to glory. I will come to visions and revelations of the Lord. I knew a man in Christ above fourteen years ago, (whether in the body, I cannot tell; or whether out of the body, I cannot tell: God knoweth;) such an one *caught up to the third heaven.* And I knew such a man, (whether in the body, or out of the body, I cannot tell: God knoweth;) How that he was *caught up into Paradise,* and heard unspeakable words, which it is not lawful for a man to utter."

We see from those precious verses that Paul did not believe the soul, spirit, and body are one, nor that they go to the grave at death, there to remain unconscious until the resurrection. He said he *knew a man* (that man was Paul himself) who was caught up into Paradise, up into the third heaven—though whether that man was IN the body or OUTSIDE the body, he did not know. Bible scholars are inclined to believe that this experience took place in Paul's life at the time he was stoned and left for dead outside the city of Lystra, but whatever the time and place of the incident, these verses plainly tell us that Paul believed the man— *the real man*—could separate from or leave the body.

There is another statement in those verses that writes Ichabod over the doctrine of soul sleep: "SUCH AN ONE CAUGHT UP TO THE THIRD HEAVEN." The grave is DOWN—but the third heaven (God's house) is UP. Paul said whether the man was in the body or outside the body, he was CAUGHT UP—not *put down* into Paradise (or into the grave,) as some would have us believe.

Paul repeats, "How that he was CAUGHT UP INTO PARADISE . . ." That Scripture plainly tells us that *Paradise is located where the third heaven is.* Verse 2 tells us that

29

such a one was caught up to the third heaven, and verse 4 repeats the fact that he was "caught UP" into *Paradise*. The *clouds* are in the *first heaven*, the *stars and planets* are in the *second heaven*, God's house is in the third heaven. ("In my Father's house are many mansions.") Paul also tells us that the man, while in Paradise, "heard unspeakable words, which it is not lawful for a man to utter." We know from this that there is talking going on NOW in Paradise.

One more verse about Paradise: "He that hath an ear, let him hear what the Spirit saith unto the churches; To him that overcometh will I give to eat of the tree of life, *which is in the midst of the Paradise of God*" (Rev. 2:7). Paradise disappears in Genesis and reappears in Revelation. The first Adam LOST Paradise; the second Adam (the Lord Jesus) bought it back (Rom. 8:18-23). Paradise is now where God is.

What are the righteous dead doing now? If we would know what the dead are doing now, there is only one place to find the answer—in the Word of God. Religions do not agree, but the Holy Scriptures agree throughout.

"And I heard a voice from heaven saying unto me, Write, Blessed (happy) are the dead which die in the Lord from henceforth; Yea, saith the Spirit, that they may rest from their labours; and their works do follow them" (Rev. 14:13).

Does that verse say to us, "Blessed are those who are unconscious in the grave"? Could it be said that a person who is unconscious or sleeping in the grave could be either blessed OR happy? "Come unto me, all ye that labour and are heavy laden, and I will give you rest. Take my yoke upon you, and learn of me; for I am meek and lowly in heart: and ye shall find rest UNTO YOUR SOULS" (Matt. 11:28,29).

God gave up flesh as being helpless, hopeless, and not worth saving in the Garden of Eden. He made no provision for saving the flesh. This mortal body will return to dust,

30

and God will give us new bodies like unto His glorious body when He comes for His church; but UNTIL He comes for His church, the *souls of* His redeemed *will rest in Paradise with Him.* "There remaineth therefore a rest to the people of God. For he that is entered into his rest, he also hath ceased from his own works, as God did from his" (Heb. 4:9,10).

"Who being the brightness of His glory, and the express image of His person, and upholding all things by the word of His power, *when He had by Himself purged our sins, sat down on the right hand of the Majesty on high*" (Heb. 1:3). Jesus is now seated at the right hand of God, and when believers are "absent from the body" they are present with Him!

"When they heard these things, they were cut to the heart, and they gnashed on (Stephen) with their teeth. But he, being full of the Holy Ghost, looked up stedfastly into heaven, and saw the glory of God, and Jesus standing on the right hand of God, and said, *Behold, I see the heavens opened, and the Son of man standing on the right hand of God.* . . . And they stoned Stephen, calling upon God, and saying, Lord Jesus, receive my spirit. And he kneeled down, and cried with a loud voice, Lord, lay not this sin to their charge. And when he had said this, *he fell asleep*" (Acts 7:54-60 in part). You will note that Stephen had already committed his spirit to the Lord—so it was only his body which fell asleep. *Jesus received the inner man.*

From these verses we learn that Stephen *"looked UP stedfastly INTO* heaven," and that He saw Jesus standing at the right hand of God—*standing* to receive Stephen's spirit.

Think on these things, beloved:

"Christ in you, the hope of glory . . ."—Col. 1:27.

"Ye are dead, and your life is hid with Christ in God

. . . "—Col. 3:3.

Through "exceeding great and precious promises" we are made partakers of Divine nature—II Peter 1:4.

"If any man have not the Spirit of Christ, he is none of His"—Rom. 8:9.

"Who shall separate us from the love of Christ?"—Rom. 8:35-39.

"Now are we the sons of God . . ."—I John 3:2.

"Grieve not the Holy Spirit of God, whereby ye are sealed unto the day of redemption"—Eph. 4:30.

"Our conversation (citizenship) is in heaven . . ."—Phil. 3:20.

"If any man be in Christ Jesus, he is a new creature . . . —II Cor. 5:17.

Any person who reads those verses and is honest with himself and with the Word of God will admit that soul-sleep is positively out of the question and foreign to the Word of God. I am not trying to defend a denomination or a religion. I am not trying to prove a point. I am simply giving *"Thus saith the Lord!"*

Where are the WICKED DEAD—and what are THEY doing now? Every wicked person who has died since the day of Adam is in hell. Referring to the wicked, the Bible says, "Terrors shall make him afraid on every side, and shall drive him to his feet . . . He shall be driven from light into darkness, and chased out of the world" (Job. 18: 11 and 18).

". . . The rich man also died, and was buried; and in hell he lift up his eyes, being in torments . . . Abraham said, Son, remember . . . NOW Lazarus is comforted, and thou ART tormented!" (Luke 16:22-25 in part). There is no suggestion of a lapse of time between the death of the rich man and his lifting up his eyes in hell. The very moment a sinner dies, that same moment he goes to hell—into the

32

flame of torment!

Some would ask, "If the wicked go to hell at death, then why the *resurrection of the wicked?*" Again the Bible is simple and plain, and will clearly teach us, if we will but look into its pages and forget the pages of doctrine written by some church or religion:

"And I saw the dead, small and great, *stand before God;* and the books were opened: and another book was opened, which is the book of life: and the dead were judged out of those things which were written in the books, according to their works. And the sea gave up the dead which were in it; and death and hell delivered up the dead which were in them: and they were judged every man according to their works. And death and hell were cast into the lake of fire. This is the second death. And whosoever was not found written in the book of life was cast into the lake of fire!" (Rev. 20:11-15).

Please notice that the dead were not judged out of the BOOK—but out of the BOOKS—the *book of life* records only the names of the redeemed; *"the books"* record the works of men. The hell in which the rich man lifted up his eyes is a temporary prison of the wicked, corresponding to the jails we know in our country. A jail is used to house a criminal behind bars until the day of his trial, and then, depending upon the seriousness of his crime, he is sent to the penitentiary to serve his sentence. Some are sentenced to serve at hard labor, some are sentenced to solitary confinement, others are given much less penalty. Such procedure is man rendering justice to man, as nearly as he knows how to mete out justice to his fellowmen. God is a just God, and He will give the wicked their just rewards. If you are cast into the lake of fire, your suffering will be to the degree of your wicked living while here on earth (Rev. 20:12,13).

33

To be consigned to hell would be terrible enough in itself, but to say that every sinner who dies will suffer the same degree of punishment throughout eternity is to do injustice to a just God! If God used the same degree of punishment for every sinner, then God would be less just than the courts of our land—and I would be afraid to accuse our Holy God of injustice.

I believe that the reasonable people who read these lines will agree that such men as Hitler, Tojo, Khrushchev and some others were men who will suffer the judgment of God. Just by way of illustration, let us use Hitler:

According to history, Hitler is dead—by his own hand. Some religionists would have us believe that Hitler is now in a state of soul-sleep; that he will sleep until the resurrection, and that he will then be raised from the dead and *burned up* with all the other wicked—and that will be the end of Hitler; Now, by contrast, take a lad who was born in a bootlegger's home, never went to Sunday school or church, never heard his dad or mother pray, never attended a revival service and knew little if anything of the great love of God. All he knew was to work at the still and make liquor. Suppose he and his dad were running from the law one night, and the lad was killed. He had never accepted Jesus, and therefore he was lost. According to the soul-sleep teachers, he is now in a state of soul-sleep, and will remain in that state until the resurrection of the wicked. At that time he will be awakened out of sleep and then along with bloody Hitler, Tojo, Mussolini and all the gangsters he will be burned up. Is that the kind of God you would have me believe my God is? Would He mete out the same degree of punishment to that poor, lost boy who never was taught about Jesus, as He would to those whose cruelty and greed wrecked nations, caused unspeakably horrible wars, tortured millions of people and committed bloody

34

slaughter wholesale? No my friend: The exceeding wicked will be rewarded in hell according to his wickedness—according to his works. The boy who might have known Jesus if his dad and mother had taken him within the sound of the Gospel also will be rewarded in hell according to his wickedness and according to the enlightenment he received while he was on earth.

You may rest assured that in heaven or in hell, mankind will receive from the hand of God exactly what it deserves—no more, and no less! And beloved, *the Bible teaches very plainly that the wicked will burn—FOREVER AND FOREVER!* The advice of Mark 9:43-48 is: ". . . If thy hand offend thee, cut it off: it is better for thee to enter into life maimed, than having two hands to go into hell, into the FIRE THAT NEVER SHALL BE QUENCHED: Where their worm dieth not, AND THE FIRE IS NOT QUENCHED. And if thy foot offend thee, cut it off: it is better for thee to enter halt into life, than having two feet to be cast into hell, into the FIRE THAT NEVER SHALL BE QUENCHED: Where their worm dieth not, and THE FIRE IS NOT QUENCHED. And if thine eye offend thee, pluck it out: it is better for thee to enter into the kingdom of God with one eye, than having two eyes to be cast into HELL FIRE: WHERE THEIR WORM DIETH NOT, AND THE FIRE IS NOT QUENCHED!"

In that passage, the Lord Jesus preached the hottest sermon on hellfire to be found in the entire Bible. Five times in those verses He says that the fires of hell will never be quenched. He did not say that they *could not be quenched* —He said that they NEVER WOULD BE quenched. The same Greek word for *everlasting* is used when referring to *everlasting life* and *everlasting punishment*. Therefore, if HELL is not eternal, then HEAVEN is not eternal! If the wicked do not *suffer forever*, the righteous do not *rejoice forever!*

35

"The same shall drink of the wine of the wrath of God, which is poured out without mixture into the cup of His indignation; and He shall be tormented with fire and brimstone in the presence of the holy angels, and in the presence of the Lamb: And the smoke of their torment ascendeth up for ever and ever: and they have no rest day nor night . . ." (Rev. 14:10,11).

"For ever and ever . . . NO REST DAY NOR NIGHT!" Does that sound like a soul *burned up?*

"And the beast was taken, and with him the false prophet that wrought miracles before him, with which he deceived them that had received the mark of the beast, and them that worshipped his image. *These both were cast alive into a lake of fire burning with brimstone"* (Rev. 19:20).

One thousand years later, at the close of the Millennium, "And the devil that deceived them was cast into the lake of fire and brimstone, *where the beast and the false prophet are,* and shall be tormented day and night for ever and ever" (Rev. 20:10).

Please note: ". . . Where the beast and the false prophet ARE!" They have been there one thousand years, they are still there, and they will be there thoroughout eternity! That does not sound like *"burning up."*

If these plain Scriptures do not convince you, dear reader, then I am afraid you will be convinced only when you wake up in hell. I hope and pray that if you are reading these lines and if you are not born again, you will bow your head right now and call on the Lord Jesus and let Him save you.

The thing uppermost in my mind in presenting this message is to help dear honest souls—and those who may be confused—to understand the difference between body, soul, and spirit; and to help them know what happens when the body dies. In these closing remarks let me sum up the

Scriptures which will set us straight—and keep us straight —if we will only believe:

Man's body was formed of the dust of the earth (Gen. 2:7), and he was no more than dust up to this point in his creation. God then breathed into his nostrils the breath of life, and man became *a living soul*. Man was but a body of dust before he became a living soul, and he BECAME a living soul ONLY when God breathed life into him.

"The Spirit of God hath made me, and the breath of the Almighty hath given me life" (Job 33:4).

"And they fell upon their faces, and said, O God, the God of the *spirits of all flesh. . . .*" (Numbers 16:22).

"And God said, Let us make man in our image, after our likeness . . . So God created man in His own image, in the image of God created He him . . ." (Gen. 1:26,27 in part).

Did this mean that God made man to favor Him in the flesh? Did it mean that we would have features like Unto God's features? No! Man is made in the image (likeness) of God in that man is a trinity.

The heavenly Trinity consists of:

1. *God the Father.* God is a spiritual being (John 4:24); God is love (I John 4:8).

2. *God the Son.* Jesus was in the bosom of the Father (John 1:18) until He was made flesh, and dwelt among us (John 1:14; Heb. 2:14). Jesus is God's gift to a lost world (John 3:16).

3. *God the Holy Spirit.* The Holy Spirit is the third Person of the Trinity. He is in the world today to comfort, lead, and seal the believer. He is here to convict the sinner and draw him to God (John 6:44; 14:16-26; 16:7-11; Rom. 8:14; Eph. 4:30).

37

The trinity of man consists of:

1. *Spirit*—the part of man which reasons and understands (I Cor. 2:11). When Jesus wept at the tomb of Lazarus he was troubled in His spirit—he was thinking and sympathizing with sorrowing sisters (John 11:33).

2. *Soul*—the seat of man's emotions; that part of man which loves or hates. In Matthew 26:38 Jesus said His soul was "exceeding sorrowful, even unto death." He was loving a lost world and pouring out His soul for sinners.

3. *Body*—the house (tabernacle) in which the spirit and soul live.

The Scriptures clearly teach that the soul, spirit, and body are separate. Paul wrote under inspiration: ". . . The very God of peace sanctify you wholly (entirely); and I pray God your whole *spirit* and *soul* and *body* be preserved blameless unto the coming of our Lord Jesus Christ" (I Thess. 5:23).

If the soul, spirit, and body are one and the same, why did not the Holy Ghost dictate to Paul in terms of *"your whole self"* or "ALL of YOU"? In Hebrews 4:12 we are told, ". . . The Word of God is quick, and powerful, and sharper than any two edged sword, piercing even to the dividing asunder of *soul* and *spirit,* and of the *joints and marrow* (*body*), and is a discerner of the thoughts and intents of the heart."

"For as the body without the spirit is dead, so faith without works is dead also" (James 2:26). Please note that it is the BODY which is dead—NOT the spirit. Man is eternal. Fifty million years from now you and I will still be living somewhere. We will either be rejoicing in the Paradise of God, or screaming in the pits of the damned!

There are those who ask, "Would a loving God permit a burning hell? Would a loving God permit His child to burn in hell?" We will answer this from the Word of God—but first let us answer from the standpoint of common sense:

Would a Christian judge permit a prison in his district? (There ARE Christian judges in our courts who fear God and who love Him.) Would such a judge turn a criminal loose and give him freedom to roam the streets of your community to molest, rob, and ravish your citizens—or would that judge send the criminal to prison or to the gas chamber? If you yourself were on a jury at the trial of a murderer, would you turn him loose to plunder and kill again—or would you vote to confine him behind prison bars?

Beloved, GOD IS LOVE—and *because* God is love, there must be a hell for those who refuse to love and serve Him. Love of decent citizens for one another is the reason we have jails and prisons—yes, and even gas chambers and electric chairs. God tells us that if a man sheds man's blood, by man shall *his* blood be shed. My home state did not build the state prison for Oliver Greene, but if Oliver Greene chooses to be a criminal and break the laws of his state, then Oliver Greene must be confined to prison—a prison not built for him, but to which he must be confined because of his actions.

By like token, God did not make hell for man. Matthew 25:41 tells us that God prepared hell for the devil and his angels. Man is not a devil, nor are evil men angels of the devil. When Lucifer rebelled against God and led some of the angels in that rebellion, God *threw Lucifer out of heaven* and *bound* the *angels,* reserving them in chains in darkness awaiting the judgment of God. Read Isaiah 14:12 ff, Ezekiel 28:1-15, and Jude 6. Genesis 1:1 tells us that "in the beginning, God created the heaven and the earth," but hell was not created at that time because there was no need for it.

Friend, if you go to hell, you will do so against the will of God. It is not His will that any should perish, but that

39

all should come to repentence (II Pet. 3:9). God has no pleasure in the death of the wicked (Ezek. 33:11). God has done everything a God of love COULD do to keep men out of hell!

If you will begin your study in Genesis 3:15 where God promised the Seed of the woman to bruise the head of the serpent, you can follow the trial of blood through every book—and almost every chapter—in the Bible—the trail of blood shed by Satan in his attempt to thwart and destroy that promised Seed. Hear the cries of little children who were brutally murdered by Satan (through ungodly men such as Pharoah and Herod). Follow the blessed Son of God from the manger to the cross—see His suffering, His scourging, His crown of thorns, His nail-pierced hands, His riven side—and hear His heart-rending cry, *"My God! My God! Why hast THOU forsaken me?"* Then read again words like these:

"Come unto me, all ye that labour, and are heavy laden, and I will give you rest."

"They that come to me I will in no wise cast out."

"How often would I have gathered thy children together, as a hen doth gather her brood under her wings, and ye would not!"

"And you will not come to Me that ye might have life."

"Believe on the Lord Jesus Christ, and thou shalt be saved."

"As many as received Him, to them gave He power to become the sons of God, even to them which believe on His name . . . which were born of God."

"By grace are ye saved through faith; and that not of yourselves: it is the Gift of God."

"That if thou shalt confess with thy mouth the Lord Jesus, and shalt believe in thine heart that God hath raised Him from the dead, thou shalt be saved."

"For whosoever shall call upon the name of the Lord shall be saved."

"If we confess our sins, He is faithful and just to forgive us our sins, and to cleanse us from all unrighteousness."

"If God be for us, who can be against us?"

"Who shall separate us from the love of God?"

"We are more than conquerors through Him that loved us."

"There hath no temptation taken you but such as is common to man: but God is faithful, who will not suffer you to be tempted above that ye are able; but will with the temptation also make a way to escape, that ye may be able to bear it."

"Greater is He that is in you, than he that is in the world."

"I will never leave thee, nor forsake thee. So that we may boldly say, The Lord is my helper, and I will not fear what man shall do unto me."

"Thanks be to God, which giveth us the victory through our Lord Jesus Christ."

"My sheep hear my voice, and a stranger they will not follow."

"Neither shall any man pluck them out of My hand."

With plain Gospel truth laid down in such plain understandable language, (and these are only a small number of such verses in the Word of God) why would anyone serve the devil, ignore God, *and go to hell?*

Yes, THERE IS A HELL—an *everlasting* hell: and all one need do to go there and suffer unspeakable torment throughout eternity is simply to *neglect God's salvation!* It is not necessary to get drunk, kill one's fellowman nor live in adultery in order to go to hell. *"To him that knoweth to do good and doeth it not, to him it is sin!"* (James 4:17). To know you *should come* to the Lord Jesus, and then *refuse*

41

to come is sin enough to send you into the lake of fire and brimstone forever.

If you are not a born again child of God, I plead with you to spend some time thinking about where you are going to spend eternity. Where will YOU go when you die? If you are a skeptic, if you doubt that there is a hereafter, if you doubt that there is a hell, then dear soul—if you cannot prove beyond a shadow of a doubt that there is no hell and no hereafter, YOU HAD BETTER PREPARE, just in case there MIGHT be a hell in the hereafter!

I beg the saved who read these lines to get out in the highways and hedges and try to get poor sinners into the ark of safety before it is everlastingly too late. I KNOW there is a hell and a hereafter. I KNOW where the dead are, and what they are doing. I am concerned about those who are "dead in trespasses and sins." I want to lead them to Jesus before they die and drop into the pits of an everlasting hell.

Five Alls

FIVE ALLS

"All grace . . . always . . . all sufficiency . . . all things . . . all good work . . ." (II Cor. 9:8).

In the original Greek, *"every"* is the word from which we get "all." There are many "alls" in the Scriptures, five of which embody the message of the Gospel.

1. *The "ALL" of sin:*

"All have sinned and come short of the glory of God" (Rom. 3:23). We are ALL in the same category. No person is without sin, nor has there *ever* been one who was free from sin. In Adam, all are born sinners. Isaiah declares, "All we like sheep have gone astray . . . and the Lord hath laid on Him the iniquity of us all" (Isa. 53:6).

Whether we study the Old Testament or the New; whether we study Genesis or Revelation, the Psalms or Matthew, we find the same grim picture: *Man* — born in sin, shapen in iniquity, wicked in his heart. "There is none that understandeth, there is none that seeketh after God. They are *all* gone out of the way, they are together become unprofitable . . ." (Rom. 3:11, 12). Without God, man is helpless, hopeless, hell-bound — and that includes ALL men!

Since *all* have sinned, what IS sin? You may rest assured that you will never get the correct answer to this question by asking preachers or religionists. Preachers do not agree on the subject, religionists do not agree on it. But the Word of God has the correct answer: "Whosoever *committeth sin transgresseth also the law: for sin is the transgression of the law"* (I John 3:4).

Almighty God has not changed His mind about His law. Heaven and earth may pass away, but not one jot or tittle of the law will ever fail. God thundered out, "Thou shalt NOT . . . !" and then, "Thou SHALT!" and He has not changed His mind. But what the law could not do in that it was weak through the flesh (Rom. 8:1-3) God sent His only begotten Son into the world in a body *like unto* sinful flesh; and in that body Jesus did what the law could never have done: He fulfilled every jot and tittle of God's law (Matt. 5:17). Therefore, "CHRIST IS THE END OF THE LAW FOR RIGHTEOUSNESS TO EVERY ONE THAT BELIEVETH" (Rom. 10:4).

The definition of sin according to the Bible is "the transgression of the law." Who would dare say he has never broken one of the commandments? And if we are guilty of the least, we are guilty of all. "By the deeds of the law there shall no flesh be justified." According to the Scriptures, we are justified by faith *without* the deeds of the law, and it is God's grace (through *faith*, not works) that saves and makes men fit for the kingdom of God.

Christ is God's perfect ideal of what man should be. Jesus came into the world on a singular mission: *To do the will of God;* and He is the only one who ever did God's will perfectly. Just before He was crucified He lifted His eyes to heaven and said, "Father . . . I have finished the work which thou gavest me to do" (John 17:4). In every minute detail of His life, ministry, and miracles; *what*ever, *when*ever, *where*ever Jesus was, His eye was single, looking to the Father — and His heart was set on doing the will of the One who sent Him.

He finished the work He came to do, He purchased redemption, He fulfilled the law. He laid His life down, He bore our sins in His own body on the cross — and he did it willingly: "No man taketh (my life) from me, but I lay it down of myself. I have power to lay it down, and I have power to take it again. This commandment have I received of my Father" (John 10:18). "Who His own self bare our sins in His own body on the tree, that we, being dead to sins, should live unto righteousness: by whose stripes ye were healed" (I Pet. 2:24).

There are those who claim that they do not need this bloody, "slaughterhouse" Gospel that talks of a Lamb on a cross and *blood* covering sin; but we are taught in the Word that "without shedding of blood is no remission" (Heb. 9:22). Since all have sinned, and since there is no remission apart from blood, then I declare without apology that each and every one of us *must be covered by the blood* — or burn in the pits of hell! Why? Because all have sinned, "the wages of sin is death," and without shedding of blood there is no remission of sin! It is the blood of Jesus that cleanses from all sin, and through His blood we have redemption — the forgiveness of sin.

Yes, ALL have sinned and come short of the glory of God. ALL we like sheep have gone astray — but God placed on Jesus the inquity of us ALL. Therefore, *"Thou* art inexcusable, O man!"* (Rom. 2:1).

2. *The "ALL" of sacrifice:*

"For there is one God, and one mediator between God and men, the man Christ Jesus; who gave Himself a ransom for ALL, to be testified in due time" (I Tim. 2:5, 6).

"A ransom for all" literally means "a procuring price." Jesus paid the price sin demanded, and the price sin demands is always singular: Whether it be king or peasant, elite or scum-bum, *the wages of sin is DEATH!* (Rom. 6:23). And when sin is finished, *it brings forth DEATH!* (James 1:15).

No one but "Himself" could pay the price. Nothing less could have satisfied God; and just as truly as nothing else *could have* satisfied God, nothing else is *needed* to satisfy God; for in Jesus, God provided what God demanded. ONLY God could have provided the sacrifice for sin.

God demands righteousness and holiness. God is God,

and the very essence of God is holiness. God cannot condone sin; He cannot acquit the wicked; He cannot look upon sin. God literally turned His head while Jesus died for the sins of the whole wide world and "gave Himself a ransom for ALL."

I am so thankful for those last words: ". . . *for ALL!* Why? If you will read some of the literature being published today, listen to some of the radio preachers who preach today, and attend some of our present day churches, you will find the answer to that question. There are many who are preaching a limited atonement — known as hyper-Calvinism (fatalism) or ultra-Predestination. Some preach that if you are elected to be saved you WILL BE saved; and if you are NOT elected, you *cannot be saved.* I believe in the sovereignty of God; God knows the end in the beginning. He is an Eternal Spirit, He is omnipotent, omniscient, and omnipresent; but that does not change the free will of man. In John 5:40 Jesus said to His own people, *"Ye will not come to me, that ye might have life!"*

My dear reader, if you burn in hell it will be your own fault — not God's. It is not God's will that any perish, but that all come to repentance (II Pet. 3:9). It is not God's will that any poor sinner die in sin and be damned for eternity in the lake of fire. John 3:16 is often referred to as "the Gospel in a nutshell": "For God so loved the world, that He gave His only begotten Son that whosoever believeth in Him should not perish, but have everlasting life." (*Whosoever* includes everyone and excludes no one!)

John 3:17 is just as precious: "For God sent not His Son into the world to condemn the world; but that the world through Him might be saved." And in I John 2:1, 2 we read, "My little children, these things write I unto you, that ye sin not, and if any man sin, we have an advocate with the Father, Jesus Christ the righteous: And He is the propitiation for our sins: and not for our's only, *but also for the sins of the whole world."*

The devil kidnapped the entire human race in the Garden of Eden. Adam sinned, although God had clearly instructed him, "The day you eat thereof, YOU DIE!" By *one man* sin entered into the world — and death by sin. So death passed upon all men, because all have sinned. However, Jesus (the second Adam) took man's place and, at the tremendous price of His blood on the cross, purchased back all that the first Adam lost in the Garden of Eden.

In the Garden of Gethsemane Jesus fought and conquered the foe that caused Adam to sell out in the Garden of Eden. Through the disobedience of Adam, the entire human race was kidnapped and *held captive* until Jesus paid the ransom with His own precious blood!

"Whosoever shall call upon the name of the Lord shall be saved" (Rom. 10:13). Never let anyone tell you that Jesus did not die for ALL sinners, or that He did not shed enough blood to pay the ransom for every sinner on the face of this earth! Jesus died for sinners — not for *a specific group* of sinners, but for ALL. Luke tells us, "For the Son of man is come to seek and to save that which was lost" (Luke 19:10). If you are lost, Jesus is seeking YOU, and He will save you if you will only hear the voice of the Spirit as He calls to you through this message.

Jesus said, "Come unto me, *all* ye that labor and are heavy laden and I will give you rest . . . Him that cometh unto me I will in no wise cast out" (Matt. 11:28 and John 6:37). His sacrifice is not for just a select, elect group, *but for ALL.* Come, believe, receive — and Jesus will save you by His marvelous grace.

3. *The "ALL" of supply:*

"What shall we then say to these things? If God be for us, who can be against us? He that spared not His own Son,

49

but delivered Him up for us all, how shall He not with Him also *FREELY give us all things?*" (Rom. 8:31, 32).

Since God so loved the world that He spared not His only begotten Son — the most precious Jewel in heaven — He (God) will not spare US anything. Those of us who believe on the Lord Jesus Christ and come to God in the name of Jesus, God will save for the sake of the Son of His love: "And be ye kind one to another, tender-hearted, forgiving one another, even as God *for Christ's sake* hath forgiven you" (Eph. 4:32).

Some have the idea that God is a monster who enjoys damning souls and seeing people fry in hell, but nothing could be further from the truth. *God is love* — God SO loved — and ONLY God *could* have so loved. Man could never do what God did: "For when we were yet without strength, in due time Christ died for the ungodly. For scarcely for a righteous man will one die: yet peradventure for a good man some would even dare to die. But God commendeth His love toward us, in that, *while we were yet sinners,* Christ died for us!" (Rom. 5:6-8).

Only GOD could love sinners enough to allow His Son to die on a cross in the sinner's place — and that is exactly what God did. Jesus paid the sin-debt with His own blood — freely and willingly — that we might be set free; and since God spared not His own Son, He will not spare us any blessing which we will receive with thanksgiving and use to the glory of our God.

"Blessed be the God and Father of our Lord Jesus Christ, who hath blessed us with all spiritual blessings in heavenly places in Christ" (Eph. 1:3).

The fifth chapter of Romans is one of my favorite portions of God's Word. In the first eleven verses of that chapter we find the seven fruits of justification — peace with God, access into His grace, glory in tribulation, etc.

50

These eleven verses close with these tremendous words: "And not only so, BUT WE ALSO JOY IN GOD THROUGH OUR LORD JESUS CHRIST, BY WHOM WE HAVE NOW RECEIVED THE ATONEMENT" (Rom. 5:11).

It is wonderful to sing about Jesus, it is wonderful to praise His name in testimony; but we should stop occasionally and bow our heads to thank God *for Himself;* because it was He who spared not His own Son. It was God who turned His head when the Son of His love cried out, "My God! My God! Why hast thou forsaken me?" It was an absolute necessity that God forsake His Son because Jesus was paying the sin-debt. Since God loved us so much, since God spared NOT His Son, He will not spare us any blessing that will make us rejoice and cause us to serve Him with thanksgiving.

God is the giver of every good and perfect gift: "Every good gift and every perfect gift is from above, and cometh down from the Father of lights, with whom is no variableness, neither shadow of turning" (James 1:17).

"And God is able to make ALL GRACE abound toward you; that ye, ALWAYS having ALL SUFFICIENCY in ALL THINGS, may abound to ALL GOOD WORK" (II Cor. 9:8).

Yes, God's grace is sufficient! Anything, everything, ALL things of which we have need, we find in His sufficiency — grace, strength, courage, temporal needs, spiritual needs — ALL are in Him.

To the Colossian believers Paul wrote that they should "walk worthy of the Lord unto all pleasing, being fruitful in every good work, and increasing in the knowledge of God; strengthened with ALL MIGHT, according to HIS glorious power, unto all patience and longsuffering with joyfulness; giving thanks unto THE FATHER, which hath made us meet to be partakers of the inheritance of the saints in light: Who (the Father) hath delivered us from the power of darkness, and hath translated us into the kingdom of His dear Son: In whom we have redemption through His blood, even the forgiveness of sins" (Col. 1:10-14).

To the believers in the church at Corinth he said, "For the Son of God, Jesus Christ, who was preached among you by us, even by me and Silvanus and Timotheus, was not yea and nay, but in Him was yea. For all the promises of God in Him are yea, and in Him Amen, unto the glory of God by us. Now he which stablisheth us with you in Christ, and hath anointed us, is God; Who hath also sealed us, and given the earnest of the Spirit in our hearts. Moreover I call God for a record upon my soul, that to spare you I came not as yet unto Corinth. Not for that we have dominion over your faith, but are helpers of your joy: for by faith ye stand" (II Cor. 1:19-24).

"THEREFORE let no man glory in men. For all things are your's!" (I Cor. 3:21). In Christ, the Son of His love, God hath given to us all blessings, all grace, all might, all promises, *all things!* With such bountiful supply we shall have plenty of all that we need — for time and for eternity.

I know no finer verse from Genesis to Revelation with which to close this "ALL" than Philippians 4:19: "But my God shall supply ALL YOUR NEED according to His riches in glory by Christ Jesus!"

4. *The "ALL" of sanctification:*

I am sometimes accused of not believing in sanctification. I confess that I do not believe in some *denominational brands* of sanctification, but I wholeheartedly believe in BIBLE sanctification. I believe that sanctification is a good, sound, fundamental Bible doctrine. Jesus said, "Sanctify them through thy Truth: Thy Word is truth" (John 17:17). "Now ye are clean through the Word which I have spoken unto you" (John 15:3).

Writing to the Corinthians, Paul gave God all glory for all things: "For ye see your calling, brethren, how that not many wise men after the flesh, not many mighty, not many noble, are called: But God hath chosen the foolish things of the world to confound the things which are mighty; and base things of the world, and things which are despised, hath God chosen, yea, and things which are not, to bring to nought things that are: That no flesh should glory in His presence. But of Him are ye in Christ Jesus, who of God is made unto us sanctification, and redemption: That, according as it is written, He that glorieth, let him glory in the Lord" (I Cor. 1:26-31).

Read and re-read these verses until you see the heart of them. Paul is very careful to point out that, in order that no flesh should ever glory in the presence of God, God made Jesus "UNTO US WISDOM, RIGHTEOUS-NESS, SANCTIFICATION, AND REDEMPTION." He closes this tremendous truth with these understandable words: "That, according as it is written, *He that glorieth, let him glory in the Lord!*"

Jesus is my sanctification; my sanctification comes through the Word; I am *clean* through the Word. God made Jesus, who knew no sin, to be sin for us, that we who believe in Him might be made righteous, holy, sanctified saints — *and that is exactly what we are, IN JESUS.* We possess the fullness of God, we are complete in Jesus, and nothing can be added to completeness: "For in Him dwelleth all the fulness of the God head bodily. And ye are complete in Him, which is the head of all principality and power" (Cor. 2:9, 10).

Writing to Titus, one of his sons in the ministry, Paul said, "For the grace of God (GOD'S grace) that bringeth salvation hath appeared to ALL men, teaching us that, denying ungodliness and worldly lusts, we should live soberly, righteously, and godly, in this present world; looking for that blessed hope, and the glorious appearing of the great God and our Saviour, Jesus Christ; *who gave Himself for us, that He might redeem us from ALL iniquity, and purify unto Himself a peculiar people, zealous of good works.* These things speak, and exhort, and rebuke with all authority. Let no man despise thee" (Titus 2:11-15).

Did you notice in this passage that God's grace appeared to *ALL men?* Jesus gave Himself that He might redeem us from *ALL iniquity.* God's minister is to speak these things, and exhort and rebuke *"with ALL authority."* A minister need not apologize for preaching grace, for preaching against ungodliness, for preaching godliness, and for admonishing people to look for Jesus, because HE is the one who gave Himself that He might redeem us from all iniquity; that He might save us, sanctify us, purify us, make us white, spotless, without wrinkle, blameless — and fit for the kingdom of God. In HIM all believers are sanctified and redeemed from ALL iniquity. (The Greek word translated "iniquity" means *lawlessness,* and lawlessness means man's self-will in opposition to God's holy will.) Man's self-will is the essence of sin — the sin of unbelief that damns; the sin of refusing to have faith in God, refusing to conform to the will of God. It is God's will that you receive Jesus and love Him with your whole heart, and all you need do to burn in hell is to neglect and reject God's love.

5. *The "ALL" of service.*

". . . WHATSOEVER ye do in word or deed, do ALL in the name of the Lord Jesus, giving thanks to God and the Father by Him" (Col. 3:17).

". . . WHATSOEVER ye do, do it heartily, as to the Lord, and not unto men" (Col. 3:23).

54

If all we say and do in all relationships of life is done in the name of the Lord Jesus Christ, then all we do will be *well done*. To act in the name of Jesus means to act as HE would act, with the authority that He would demonstrate and declare; to speak in His name in all sincerity is to speak as Jesus would speak.

In I Corinthians 10:31 Paul says, "Whether therefore ye eat, or drink, or WHATSOEVER ye do, do ALL to the glory of God." The believer has no right to do anything for self (with a selfish motive), because we are not our own. We are bought with a price, and it is the command of God that we glorify Him in body, in spirit, and all that we do:

"What? Know ye not that your body is the temple of the Holy Ghost which is in you, which ye have of God, and ye are not your own? For ye are bought with a price: therefore glorify God in your body, and in your spirit, which are God's" (I Cor. 6:19, 20).

There is only one Foundation, and that Foundation is Jesus Christ, our Lord. He is the stone which the builders disallowed, whom God has made the chief cornerstone. He is the rock upon which God is building the church. He is the head of the church, He is the Saviour of the body, and every born again child of God is a member of that body (I Cor. 12:12, 13). We are His purchased property; we are His building: we have no right to our own desires or wishes. Our very existence should be dedicated to a singular purpose — that of glorifying God in every phase of our living, thinking, acting, or speaking. In all our ways we should acknowledge Him. In all of our living we should glorify Him, remembering that we are not our own. We are purchased with a price — *His precious blood!*

Redemption is free. Salvation is the gift of God. *By God's grace we are saved:* "Not by works of righteousness which we have done, but according to His mercy He hath saved us." When we confess with our mouth and believe in our hearts that God raised Jesus from the dead, He saves us. With the heart we believe unto righteousness, and with the mouth we confess salvation.

Reward is another matter. We will be rewarded for faithful stewardship, faithful service — not so much the amount of service, but what SORT it is:

"Now if any man build upon this foundation gold, silver, precious stones, wood, hay, stubble; every man's work shall be made manifest: for the day shall declare it, because it shall be revealed by fire; and the fire shall try every man's work of WHAT SORT it is. If any man's work abide which he hath built thereupon, he shall receive a reward. If any man's work shall be burned, he shall suffer: but he himself shall be saved; yet so as by fire. Know ye not that ye are the temple of God, and that the Spirit of God dwelleth in you? If any man defile the temple of God, him shall God destroy; *for the temple of God is holy, which temple ye are"* (I Cor. 3:12-17).

It is extremely important that believers understand the New Testament teaching concerning stewardship and reward. Whatsoever we do in word or in deed, we should do it ALL in the name of the Lord Jesus. And if whatsoever we do is NOT done in the name of Jesus to the glory of God it will be wood, hay, stubble — and it will be burned! What kind of steward am I? What kind of steward are *you?*

Yes, ALL have sinned and come short of the glory of God, but Jehovah laid upon His beloved Son the iniquities of us ALL. Jesus (the spotless Lamb) willingly and freely gave Himself, a ransom for ALL. He paid the price, He purchased our redemption.

Since God so loved us that He permitted Jesus to pay the ransom, then *through Jesus* God freely gives us ALL

56

things. All that we need, we find in Him — spiritual needs, physical needs, the needs of time and eternity. In Jesus we have redemption from ALL iniquity. In Him we are justified, purified, spotless, blameless, sanctified and holy. God gave Jesus to redeem us from all iniquity.

It is our solemn duty that whatsoever we do or say, whether much or little, we do or say it ALL in the name of the Lord Jesus Christ to the glory of the Father who so loved us that He gave the Son of His love to die on the cruel cross for us, that we might have life and have it abundantly.

I close this message with the words of the man of wisdom, found in Ecclesiastes 12:13 and 14: *"Let us hear the conclusion of the whole matter: FEAR GOD, and keep His commandments: FOR THIS IS THE WHOLE DUTY OF MAN."* (Please note: "The WHOLE DUTY." Yes, it is a grand and glorious privilege to serve God, but it is also a divine duty.) "For God shall bring every work into judgment, with every secret thing, whether it be good, or whether it be evil."

Are you saved? If not, will you not bow your head right now, and in these simple words invite Jesus to save you: "Lord Jesus, I confess my need of a Saviour. I confess that I have sinned. I know the wages of sin is death. Forgive my sin, cover my sins with the precious blood, and save me, for Jesus' sake. I receive Jesus as my Saviour NOW! Lord Jesus, come into my heart and *save me now*. Thank you, Jesus, for saving my soul! Amen."

Our Salvation Incorruptible

OUR SALVATION INCORRUPTIBLE

One of the greatest needs today among church people is to recognize the difference between "religion" and **salvation.** There is much confusion concerning genuine redemption through the shed blood of the Lord Jesus Christ. There is a great revival of "religion," a great revival of "church joining," but there is a vast difference between **possessing salvation** and having one's name on a local church roll.

I would like to point out six things about salvation:

1. **Our salvation is provided by the one "incorruptible God."**

In the first chapter of Romans, Paul describes the seven stages of Gentile world apostasy. He declares that when people knew God they refused to glorify Him AS God. They were unthankful, they became vain in their imagination and their foolish hearts were darkened. They professed to be wise and became fools. All of this led to rank idolatry, "and changed the glory of THE INCORRUPTIBLE GOD into an image made like to corruptible man, and to birds, and fourfooted beasts, and creeping things. Wherefore God also gave them up to uncleanness through the lusts of their own hearts" (Rom. 1:23-24).

In this passage Paul clearly points out that our God is incorruptible—and if God is incorruptible, then He is eternal and can never cease to be. God is sovereign; He has been FROM everlasting and will be TO everlasting (Psalm 90:1-2). God is eternal, He cannot pass away; He has always been and always will be. Salvation provided by an eternal, incorruptible God is also incorruptible, eternal, and cannot pass away. We are saved with an eternal salvation.

It was God who so loved the world that He gave His only begotten Son to die on the cross for sinners (John 3:16). It was God who turned His head as His Son cried out, "My

God, My God, why hast thou forsaken me!" (Mark 16:34). And as the Father turned away, the Son willingly paid the sin-debt. If the Father had so willed to call His Son down from the cross, you and I would burn in hell forever because it had to be Jesus who paid the sin-debt for us. Jesus was God's only begotten Son—yea, God in flesh (II Cor. 5:19).

When Jesus prayed in the Garden, "If it be possible, let this cup pass—nevertheless, not as I will, but as Thou wilt," if God the Father had removed the cup . . . if He had forbidden the Lord Jesus to drink that cup . . . then you and I would spend eternity in hell because there was no other to pay sin's debt (Matt. 26:39). Therefore, God provided our salvation. It was God who loved so much that He was willing to surrender the Son of His love and permit Him to die the most horrible, shameful death known to man, that we might have salvation and eternal life!

Through John, the Holy Spirit sums it up clearly and in words easily understood: "And this is the record, that God hath given to us eternal life, and this life is in His Son, He that hath the Son hath life; and he that hath not the Son of God hath not life" (I John 5:11-12). That settles it! God has given to us eternal life; He has given us salvation and this salvation is in His Son. Since Jesus is our salvation, then our salvation is incorruptible and cannot be destroyed by all the forces of hell plus the devil himself. We have an incorruptible salvation through the incorruptible gift given to us by the incorruptible God—His own Son, begotten of God.

2. **All who possess salvation by faith in the finished work of the Lord Jesus are covered with His "incorruptible blood."**

"Forasmuch as ye know that ye were not redeemed with corruptible things, as silver and gold, from your vain conversation received by tradition from your fathers: BUT WITH THE PRECIOUS BLOOD OF CHRIST, AS OF A LAMB WITHOUT BLEMISH AND WITHOUT SPOT" (I Peter 1:18-19).

In these precious verses we learn that our redemption was not wrought through any medium that can corrupt—not by "corruptible things, as silver and gold." If our redemption is not wrought with things that can corrupt, if our redemption is by and through "the precious blood of Christ," then the blood of Christ is incorruptible, the simple argument being that anything that can corrupt cannot redeem the soul. Salvation in Christ therefore provides an incorruptible covering by and through the incorruptible blood of the Lord Jesus Christ.

Never entertain the idea that the blood of Jesus Christ dripped from His hands and feet onto the rocks of Calvary to be dried by the sun and carried away by insects! The blood that flowed through the veins of the Son of God was incorruptible; it could not decay. His blood did not perish— **and shall not.**

"Take heed therefore unto yourselves, and to all the flock, over that which the Holy Ghost hath made you overseers, to feed the church of God, which He hath purchased with His own blood!" (Acts 20:28).

The Virgin Mary was the mother of Jesus; God Almighty was His Father. The life is in the blood; and if Jesus was conceived by the power of the Holy Ghost, Jehovah God being His Father, then the life that pulsated through His veins was the blood of Almighty God. Understand it? NO! Accept it? YES! God said it, I believe it: "Let God be true, and every man a liar" (Rom. 3:4). I am happy that the redemption I have—the redemption that will protect me when I stand before God in all of His holiness—is beyond man's understanding.

63

Salvation is received by faith—not accepted through man's wisdom nor his ability to **understand** God's salvation. We are covered with a covering that cannot corrupt. When we stand before God, the blood is our guarantee of hearing Him say, "Enter thou into the joys of thy Lord."

3. **Salvation provided by the incorruptible God through the incorruptible blood of His only begotten Son becomes ours by the power of the incorruptible Word.**

In John 3:5 Jesus said to Nicodemus, "Verily, verily, I say unto thee, Except a man be born of water and of the Spirit, he cannot enter the kingdom of God." The new birth is a divine imperative; without it there is no salvation.

Peter enlightens us as to the "how" of the new birth: "Being born again, not of corruptible seed, but of incorruptible, by the Word of God, which liveth and abideth for ever" (I Peter 1:23). Here we learn of the power through which we are born into God's family.

Paul said to the Romans, "I am not ashamed of the Gospel . . . it is the power of God unto salvation . . ." Jesus said, "Verily, verily, I say unto you, He that heareth my word and believeth on Him that sent me, hath everlasting life, and shall not come into condemnation; but is passed from death unto life" (John 5:24). The Word of God is the seed that brings forth the new birth. The Word of God is incorruptible; therefore when we are born of God we live forever.

Notice carefully: "Being born again, NOT OF CORRUPTIBLE SEED, but of incorruptible, by the Word of God, which liveth and abideth for ever." Therefore when the seed (the Word) is planted in our hearts and, mixed with faith, springs up into everlasting life, the seed produces salvation—everlasting, eternal life. Never forget: "This life is in His Son" (I John 5:11-12).

"In the beginning was the Word, and the Word was with

God, and the Word was God" (John 1:1). Remember the Word is the incorruptible seed that brings salvation.

Again, "The Word was made flesh, and dwelt among us, (and we beheld His glory, the glory as of the only begotten of the Father,) full of grace and truth" (John 1:14). The Word in flesh was Jesus; Jesus is the Son of God's love, given for us that we might be saved—"Christ in you, the hope of glory."

"There is therefore now no condemnation to them which are in Christ Jesus." When we possess Jesus we possess the incorruptible Word, and we have within us the divine nature of the incorruptible God (II Peter 1:4). When we have within us the divine nature of the incorruptible God we possess salvation that cannot corrupt, decay, or pass away. Thank God for the incorruptible Word that makes us wise unto salvation! Faith comes by hearing and hearing by the Word. Therefore the Word brings to our heart saving faith (Rom. 10:17).

4. All who possess salvation have an incorruptible inheritance.

"Blessed be the God and Father of our Lord Jesus Christ, which according to His abundant mercy hath begotten us again unto a lively hope by the resurrection of Jesus Christ from the dead, to an inheritance incorruptible, and undefiled, and that fadeth not away, reserved in heaven for you, who are kept by the power of God through faith unto salvation ready to be revealed in the last time" (I Peter 1:3-5).

Our inheritance at the end of life's journey is incorruptible, and that inheritance begins the moment we put our faith and trust in Jesus. As we are faithful stewards serving Him with faithfulness day by day we add to that inheritance, because every believer will be rewarded according to his faithful stewardship (I Cor. 3:11-15). The salvation that we possess (provided by the incorruptible God, our covering being the incorruptible blood made ours through the power of the incorruptible Word,) assures us that we have an incorruptible inheritance, a home in heaven that will not corrupt, decay, nor pass away, reserved in heaven for those of us "who are kept by the power of God through faith."

In this life it is altogether possible to be rich today and poor tomorrow; to have a beautiful home today and only ashes tomorrow. But thank God, the home Jesus is preparing for the saints is a home that cannot be destroyed, yea, **shall not** be destroyed, a home incorruptible—eternal in the city of God.

5. **Born again believers who are faithful will wear an incorruptible crown.**

Paul illustrates this truth through the games and races of his day. The Greeks were known for athletic prowess and sports, and in I Corinthians 9:25 Paul uses terms with which the people of that day were familiar: "And every man that striveth for the mastery is temperate in all things. Now they do it to obtain a corruptible crown; but we an incorruptible."

This Scripture simply tells us that the young men who run such races in order that they may win a crown, abstain from lusts and habits that will tear down their bodies; but the crown won in those races will corrupt, while the crown Jesus gives to those who run a good race in the spiritual realm is incorruptible. Those who present their bodies a living sacrifice, holy, acceptable unto God, and who run the race to God's glory, pointing others to the Lamb of God, at the end of a life of faithful stewardship **will wear a crown that will never corrupt.** Bear in mind that anything with which God has to do CANNOT corrupt. An incorruptible God could not produce corruptible things.

6. Last but by no means least—**all who possess true salvation will receive a body that will never corrupt.**

Writing to the Corinthian church, Paul said, "Behold, I shew you a mystery; we shall not all sleep, but we shall all be changed. In a moment, in the twinkling of an eye, at the last trump: for the trumpet shall sound, and the dead shall be raised incorruptible, and we shall be changed. For this corruptible must put on incorruption, and this mortal must put on immortality" (I Cor. 15:51-53).

"For we know that if our earthly house of this tabernacle (body) were dissolved, we have a building of God, an house not made with hands, eternal in the heavens . . . (For we walk by faith, not by sight:) We are confident, I say, and willing rather to be absent from the body, and to be present with the Lord" (II Cor. 5: 1, 7, 8).

John describes our eternal body in I John 3:2: "Beloved, now are we the sons of God, and it doth not yet appear what we shall be: but we know that, when He shall appear, WE SHALL BE LIKE HIM; FOR WE SHALL SEE HIM AS HE IS."

To all this I say, "Hallelujah! Thank God for His incorruptible, undying love!"

True salvation was provided in the eternity behind us because of the love of THE INCORRUPTIBLE GOD, who so loved that He permitted His only begotten Son to give His incorruptible blood that we might be redeemed by that blood. Jesus was the incorruptible Word in flesh. He brought God down to man, that we might know the truth about God who loved us, and knowing the truth we might be set free from sin and death (John 8:32).

The incorruptible Word, wrapped in the flesh given to Jesus by the Virgin Mary, tabernacled among men and made known to them the way of life. To Thomas Jesus said, "I am the way, the truth, and the life: no man cometh unto the Father but by me" (John 14:6). All who accept the incorruptible Word will inherit an incorruptible inheritance that cannot—yea, SHALL NOT—pass away. We will wear an incorruptible crown, we will live forever in our incorruptible body . . . a body just like the glorious resurrection body of Jesus.

The most reasonable thing any person has ever done or ever will do is to hear the Word of God and receive the salvation provided by Him through the death of His only begotten Son. Remember the words of John: "And this is the record, that God hath given to us eternal life, and this life is in His Son. He that hath the Son hath life; and He that hath not the Son of God hath not life" (I John 5:11-12).

Perfect Peace

PERFECT PEACE

"Thou wilt keep him in perfect peace, whose mind is stayed on thee: because he trusteth in thee" (Isaiah 26:3).

These are days when we hear much about peace—world peace, lasting peace. We hear statements such as "Help us to keep the peace!" The truth of the matter is, the only place where there IS peace today is in the heart of the believer.

Peace is the exact opposite of strife, discord, and conflict. All one need do is stop, look, and listen. Anyone can readily see that we are living in an age of strife, discord, and opposition . . . religiously, politically, and in every way. Since peace is the opposite of discord, peace denotes harmony, accord, oneness. When having to do with the individual, peace signifies a state of wholeness, completeness, health, and well–being—spiritually, physically, and mentally.

We derive our word "peace" from the Hebrew word **"Shalom,"** which means completeness, wholeness, oneness. The word signifies **much** peace, **great** peace, an **abundance of peace,** hence the words in our text, **"perfect peace."** This perfect peace of which we speak must come from the perfect God. No one BUT the perfect God could supply perfect peace. Through the perfect sacrifice of Christ's atonement, God provided perfect peace for all who will receive peace **on the terms of the Gospel.**

God, through the perfect sacrifice of Christ's atonement, assured by the perfect Word of the Spirit's assurance—enjoyed by the God-given grace of faith, such faith becoming ours by hearing the Word of the God of perfect peace, the peace of God becomes ours when we exercise faith in the finished work of Jesus—His shed blood through which and only through which peace can be enjoyed by the individual.

In this age of psychiatry and pills, institutions are provided for repairing nerves and minds, and such institutions

71

are crowded and running over. Surely this perfect peace is needed and should be sought after by all who hear the glorious message that such peace **can abide** in the bosom of each and every person who will accept God's gift of peace on the terms of the Gospel.

Such peace can become yours and mine only according to the terms of the Gospel. The Creator has an unquestioned right to legislate for that which He has created, and we know that God created man in His own image, breathed into his nostrils the breath of life, and man became a living soul. Therefore, God has a perfect right to declare by and through what means we may become recipients of His eternal blessings. God has devised the plan of salvation through His own begotten Son, the Lord Jesus Christ, and has positively declared that there is salvation in no other; there is no other name under heaven given among men whereby we must be saved. Anyone who devises his own plan of salvation disbelieves or distrusts the plan provided by God. Such unbelief strikes a direct blow at God the Father and pours contempt upon His sovereignty, doubting His wisdom in providing salvation according to the Scriptures.

1. Perfect peace is blood-purchased.

"And, having made peace through the blood of His cross, by Him to reconcile all things unto Himself; by Him, I say, whether they be things in earth, or things in heaven" (Col. 1:20).

"Forasmuch as ye know that ye were not redeemed with corruptible things . . . BUT WITH THE PRECIOUS BLOOD OF CHRIST, as of a lamb without blemish and without spot" (I Pet. 1:18, 19).

Peace with God is not a product of man's wisdom and ability. Before ever the universe was brought into being, before the creation of man, God settled the "how" and "who" of peace with Him. Perfect peace is not a product of earth. It is not an obtainment of man's ability and endeavor, nor is it a bestowment of man's giving. Perfect peace is not a priceless gem of man's finding, nor a virtue brought by angels. It is not a diamond mined from earth's terrain, nor is it the outcome of the magician's art. **Perfect peace is provided by God** — and ONLY by God, through Christ's blood.

Jesus did for God the Father what man could never have done. He finished the work God sent Him to do, thereby providing the perfect peace that only a perfect God **could** provide. The imperfection of man could never provide perfection; hence, Christ has given to God for us what we ourselves could never give through our wisdom or ability.

"THEREFORE being justified by faith, we have peace with God through our Lord Jesus Christ: by whom also we have access by faith into this grace wherein we stand, and reoice in hope of the glory of God" (Rom. 5:1, 2).

When Adam sinned, fellowship between God and man was broken; warfare began, and continued until the Man Christ Jesus bought back all that Adam had lost. The second Adam, in a body of flesh, purchased perfect peace between God and man at the price of His blood. Jesus was God in flesh (II Cor. 5:19) and therefore He, the second Adam, was the God whom man offended, in the man who offended Him. Jesus was the Offended and the offender in one body, and in that body of flesh He provided redemption, justification, and peace—peace that only Jesus could have provided because man had failed and sinned. God demands perfection, holiness, and righteousness; and the seed of Adam could produce no better than the seed from whence it came. But Jesus was more than man—He was God in flesh; and in that body of flesh He did what man could never have done. Therefore, we enjoy the blood-purchased peace—perfect peace.

2. **Perfect peace is faith-obtained.**

73

"Therefore being justified by faith, we have peace with God through our Lord Jesus Christ" (Rom. 5:1).

THEREFORE takes us back to Romans 4:25: "Who was delivered for (on account of) our offences, and was raised again for (on account of) our justification." Since Jesus was delivered on account of our offences, when we believed on Him and put our faith in His finished work, our faith is accounted for righteousness. **Our sin being reckoned to Christ, Christ the righteousness of God is therefore reckoned to us**.

When Esther went into the presence of king Ahasuerus, she was not at all sure of the king's mind toward her; she did not know how he would receive her. She said, "If I perish, I perish . . ." but when she appeared in the presence of the king, he in grace held out to her the golden sceptre and she touched it with the hand of faith, knowing that the king's favor toward her was granted.

Esther went in to stand before the king with uncertainty, but **there is no uncertainty concerning God's favor to us**. The grace and love of God are extended toward us in the extended hands of Christ on the cross, taking our sins, pleading for our iniquities; and the moment we take Him by faith as our Saviour, we receive the benefit of His shed blood and His atoning death. He bore our sins in His own body on His cross; He purchased our redemption at the tremendous price of His blood. Just before He literally passed His Spirit back to the heavenly Father, He said, "It is finished (It is accomplished) . . . Father, into thy hands I commend my Spirit!" and gave up the ghost.

God deals in faith: We are saved by grace through faith (Eph. 2:8). The just shall live by faith (Rom. 1:17). We overcome the world by faith (I John 5:4); and **"Whatsoever is not of faith is sin"** (Rom. 14:23). Faith is the hand of need that reaches out to receive the Lord's blessings (Mark 5:24-34). Faith is the machinery of work, love is the power

74

which moves it, and hope is the outcome of faith and love (Gal. 5:5, 6). Faith opens the heart's door to Christ; love dwells in the heart of appreciation for Christ, and hope expects the fulfillment of every promise made by the Lord Jesus Christ (Eph. 3:17-19). Faith is characterized by work; faith without works is dead. Love is characterized by labor, and hope by patience (I Thess. 1:3). Faith and love form the breastplate of protection for the believer, and hope is the helmet of salvation (I Thess. 5:8). Faith is coupled with righteousness, love provides godliness, and hope produces meekness (I Tim. 6:8-11). Faith ascends the stirs which love has provided, and then looks out of the window which hope has opened. In Mark 11:22 Jesus said to His disciples, "Have faith in God," and Hebrews 11:6 tells us, "Without faith it is impossible to please God."

3. Perfect peace is Christ-pledged.

"Peace I leave with you, my peace I give unto you: not as the world giveth, give I unto you. Let not your heart be troubled, neither let it be afraid" (John 14:27).

In this tremendous verse, **double peace** is clearly pointed out: Here we have the legacy of the dying Saviour to whomsoever will become a recipient of perfect peace through faith in His finished work: **"PEACE I LEAVE WITH YOU."** But we also have the gift of our gracious Lord: **"MY PEACE I give unto you."**

God created man in His own image, and man cannot know perfect peace until he comes into the right relationship with God, his Creator; nor can he know perfect rest until he is yoked with the Lord Jesus. Jesus said, "Come unto me, all ye that labor and are heavy laden, and I will give you rest." But He went further than that and gave a command: **"Take my yoke upon you."** (The literal Greek reads, "Take the yoke with me in the will of God, and ye shall find rest unto your souls"—Matt. 11:28, 29).

Peace with God and rest to the entire life of the individual are possible only as that individual is yoked with Christ in God's will. There is no real well-**being** except by **being well** within the will of God; and the only way to be in the will of God is to trust Jesus in all things without wavering, relying completely on Him—not only for eternity, but for time as well; not only for spirit and soul, but for body and physical well-being. We are to trust Him in all things, at all times, under all circumstances, knowing that He is able and willing to do exceeding abundantly above anything that we think or ask. He came that we might have life, and that we might have it abundantly. The birthright of every child of God is "perfect peace, full assurance, and perfect rest," but very few believers enjoy their spiritual birthright.

Let me repeat for emphasis: **GOD DEALS IN FAITH**. We are saved by God's grace, and saving grace becomes ours through faith. "The just shall live by faith"—not by sight or feelings. Faith is the victory that overcomes the world, and whatsoever is not of faith is sin.

The testimony of true faith is: "He bore my sins in His own body on the tree" (I Pet. 2:24). Faith sings from the heart, "He loved me and gave Himself for me" (Gal. 2:20). Faith that brings salvation emphasizes the death of Christ on the cross as the starting point of the Christian life. Paul said, "For I delivered unto you first of all that which I also received, how that Christ died for our sins according to the Scriptures; and that He was buried, and that He rose again the third day according to the Scriptures" (I Cor. 15:3, 4).

The death of the Lord Jesus Christ is the starting point, the very heart and essence of life eternal; and **apart from His death** there could have been no salvation. "We love Him, because He first loved us" (I John 4:19). "I shall be satisfied when I awake with (His) likeness" (Psalm 17:15). We know that Jesus, "having loved His own, loved them to the end" (John 13:1). Those of us whom God loved and who have exercised faith in the shed blood of His only begotten Son, are "kept by the power of God through faith unto salvation" (I Pet. 1:5).

In this message we have learned that perfect peace is possible to the individual who will yield unreservedly to God. Perfect peace is blood-purchased, faith-obtained, and Christ-pledged—and thank God, **the pledge is made by one who cannot lie** (Heb. 6:18; Titus 1:2). Every good gift and every perfect gift comes from the Lord, and it is God's good pleasure to withhold no good thing from them that walk uprightly. Jesus came that we might have life and have it abundantly, and the **fullness** of the life Jesus gives will be experienced when He comes again for His own: "When Christ, WHO IS OUR LIFE, shall appear, then shall (we) also appear with Him in glory" (Col. 3:4). As we travel this pilgrim journey, IN the world but not OF it, we can possess and enjoy perfect peace, unshakable assurance, and hope that removes all fear of living, fear of dying, and fear of standing before a holy God!

Do YOU have peace with God? If not, you can obtain that peace through faith in the finished work of Jesus—His death, His burial, His resurrection. Bow your head and in your own words ask Him to save you, confessing to Him that you need a Saviour—and He will save you now!

"Believe on the Lord Jesus Christ, and thou shalt be saved, and thy house" (Acts 16:31).

"Very, verily, I say unto you, He that heareth my word, and believeth on Him that sent me, hath everlasting life, and shall not come into condemnation: but is passed from death unto life" (John 5:24).

Hear the Word, believe the Word, receive the Lord Jesus Christ by faith, and He will save you now.

Rub It In

RUB IT IN

In the Sermon on the Mount, the Lord Jesus said to His disciples, *"Ye are the salt of the earth!"* (Matt. 5:13).

Many sermons have been preached on this text, all of them using approximately the same three points: (1) Salt *seasons* — about ten minutes are used to develop that line of thought. (2) Salt *purifies* — about ten minutes are allotted to that point. (3) Salt *preserves* — perhaps five minutes are used to elaborate on this one. That adds up to about twenty-five minutes, and the average congregation cannot stand *more* than twenty-five minutes of preaching. (Of course, most of them would not tire of watching a double-feature at the theatre or on television.)

But as many times as I have heard the above text used, I do not recall ever hearing or reading a message that includes the *fourth* point: *SALT IRRITATES!* Jesus said to His followers, "Ye are the salt of the earth." Those early disciples were salty — and what effect did they have upon those with whom they came in contact? Did they only season, purify, and preserve those with whom they had to do?

If you will read the Book of Acts and some of the epistles you will find that they also *irritated* some who heard them. Salt irritates, and those men made no attempt to keep from "rubbing it in!" They were often arrested, they were threatened, they were beaten and dragged outside the city for dead. They were forbidden to speak again in the name of Jesus — but none of those things could cause these giants of faith to become "good mixers" or to change the doctrine that made them "salty" and irritating to the crowd of religionists of their day.

When the religious rulers brought those first Christians in for questioning, the answers given were not soft-spoken answers from hearts of fear toward man, but BOLD answers which came from hearts that feared only God. *"We cannot but speak the things which we have seen and heard,"* they replied; or, *"Which is better—to obey God, or man?"* And when those street-preaching men of Galilee were gone out from them, the religious bosses *"took knowledge that they had been with Jesus!"*

I wonder how many sinners, after having been in your presence and mine, take knowledge that we have been with Jesus? I wonder what our answer would be if some of the big denominational bosses should come to us and demand that we never again speak publicly in the name of Jesus Christ? Oh, I know we SAY we would do this, or that — but since we are doing so little as it is, I wonder what we would *really* do in the face of such opposition?

Real, blood-bought Christianity rubs the world the wrong way! The "cold stream" religion predominant in the land today soothes rather than irritates the world. Someone said, "If I preach rough, rugged Gospel, it will rub my congregation the wrong way." Friend, if rough, rugged Gospel rubs a congregation the wrong way, they need to *turn around* — and then it will rub them the *right* way! There is nothing wrong with pure, plain Gospel. It is the "cream-puff" religion which most church members have today that causes them to be irritated by the kind of preaching done by John the Baptist.

Jesus instructed His disciples (including you and me) to take His yoke upon us, come alongside Him, walk in His steps, and preach as He preached. If we do that we will preach repentance or damnation: *". . . Except ye repent, ye shall all likewise perish!"* (Luke 13:3-5). If we preach as Jesus preached, we will preach *hell fire* (Matt. 5:22, 29, 30); and we will preach *separation*. Jesus plainly told His disciples, "And whosoever shall not receive you, nor hear your words, when ye depart out of that house or city, shake off the dust of your feet" (Matt. 10:14, also Luke 9:5).

The cry today is "Fellowship! Fellowship! Fellowship! Bring in the modernists, the agnostics, the liberals — and all the rest! Come, let us fellowship together!" But what did our Saviour say about fellowship? *"Can two walk together except they be agreed?"* (Amos 3:3). "Wherefore come ye out from among them, and be ye separate, saith the Lord . . . " (II Cor. 6:17). Jesus said of His disciples, "I have given them (my) Word; and the world hath hated them, because they are not of the world, even as I am not of the world" (John 17:14). The idea of fellowshipping with liberals, modernists, and every "ism, schism, and spasm" of this broad-minded religious age originated in hell — not in heaven nor in the Bible!

"Yea, and all that will live godly in Christ Jesus shall suffer persecution" (II Tim. 3:12). Godly living is a rebuke to this age. When a person announces that he believes in the verbal inspiration of the Scriptures, believes in a church separated from worldliness, modernism, and compromise, that person is looked upon as being "narrow, un-co-operative, and holier-than-thou," when in actuality all the dear believer is trying to do is to carry out God's command to be "salty"! The modern church resents and is irritated by the light of the Gospel which exposes its corruption — corruption being carried on in the name of religion!

Jesus drove the money-changers and their animals from the temple in Jerusalem. I wonder what this same Jesus would do today, should He walk in on the "well-chaperoned" dances, bingo games and rummage sales being held in church basements and recreation parlors in the name

83

of religion? You may think what you like, but since Jesus is the same — yesterday, today, forever — I personally believe that if no cords were available from which He could make a whip, He would pick up a broom or a mop handle and there would be a "scattering time!" He would overturn the jukebox which furnishes music for church dances. He would overturn the tables on which food is being served to feed already fat church members. And I believe His comment would be no less severe than when He overturned the tables of the money-changers in Jerusalem!

The church of the living God is to be a testimony to poor, lost sinners. But under the modern program we are told to fellowship with unbelievers, invite liberals and modernists to sit on our platforms, speak in our churches— and we are expected to take part in their suppers and parties in order to prove to them that we are Christians! Jesus called them hypocrites, blind guides, fools; whited sepulchres full of dead men's bones (read Matthews 23).

We are to love the poor lost souls of these people — yes; but we are to "come out from among them . . . and have no fellowship with the unfruitful works of darkness." Jesus warned us that times like these would surely come in the last days. He warned that false prophets would arise, and would deceive many. He pointed out the danger of these false teachers: *"Beware of false prophets, which come to you in sheep's clothing, but inwardly they are ravening wolves"* (Matt. 7:15).

The visible church today is full of such "wolves" — most of them not only parading in sheep's clothing, but also having a sheepskin diploma from some modernistic school or university! They sneak in unaware, like thieves (which is what they are — John 10:1) trying to tell lost souls that they can get to heaven without the blood-bought salvation of the Lord Jesus.

84

These preachers are spoken of in II Timothy 3:7 as "ever learning, and never able to come to the knowledge of the truth." They are trained by the universities and colleges of the denominational machines and are brought into the churches by the denominational bosses. They know what they are supposed to preach and they dare not move without orders from headquarters. They are instructed to be "good mixers," and to preach "the fatherhood of God and the brotherhood of man." They are told to shy away from the old-time, "slaughterhouse" religion; so the first thing they do is tear out the altar, throw out the old-fashioned mourner's bench, and set up a card-signing, hand-shaking, big membership campaign. They bring in anybody and everybody who will *come* in, (many of them from the crowd the old-fashioned "salty" preachers ran off.) They set up the machinery to run the church like the "membership" crowd wants to run it, and if a leader perchance objects to such practice he is railroaded out and one of the "fellowshippers" takes his place!

These assembly-line preachers who took up preaching as a "profession" want a church which stands high in the opinion of all the lovely folk of the community — the theatre owners, the tavern operators, the nightclub owners, and possibly even the liquor store owners! They want to get them into the church ("and then they will be in a position to be helped," they say.) But the Bible plan has not changed: As in Acts 2:47, *the Lord still adds to the church such as are being saved.*

The modern preacher is instructed never to preach a gospel that would offend the liberals and modernists. "Fellowship is the thing — get them into the church, get them on the membership roll. They are good folks; they just do not see things like the old-fashioned, mourners' bench Christians saw them." That is true — and they will never see the HEAVEN which the old-fashioned, mourners' bench Christians go to, either!

Modernists are trying to develop a brand of religion which will not *irritate the world* — a brand of religion which will not offend the Sunday morning worshipper who lives like the devil the rest of the week! In one city where I was holding a revival meeting, one fashionable pastor put a notice in the paper which read, "Beginning Sunday, we will have a service at eight, and another at eleven o'clock A.M., in order that those who desire to get an early start to the beach may attend the early service and still reach the beach before the noon hour. By so doing, they can worship God and enjoy a peaceful Sunday at the beach!" The same article went on to say that this church age does not adhere to the Puritan way of observing Sunday. (God is the same God today as in the days of the Puritans, and according to His Word, these modernists are not going to the heaven where the Puritans went, either!)

Sad but true, religion in this country is becoming "big business." All some preachers care about is that the congregation come to church long enough to put in their weekly pledge — but that is not all the Lord Jesus cares about. The whole duty of man is to fear God and keep His commandments (Ecc. 12:13). We are to love God with all our heart, soul, mind and strength. A religion minus love and devotion to the Lord Jesus is a vain religion.

Jesus said something else about salt: "But *if the salt have lost his savour*, wherewith shall it be salted? It is thenceforth good for nothing, but to be cast out, and to be trodden under foot of men!"

Whether it be table salt or spiritual salt — salt which has lost its savor is GOOD FOR NOTHING! Just so, religion which has lost its savor is good for nothing—in fact, the heathen are much better off in God's sight. The Word of God plainly tells us, "That servant, which *knew* his lord's will, and prepared not himself, *"neither did according to his will,* shall be beaten with *many* stripes. But he that *knew not,* and did commit things worthy of stripes, shall be beaten with *few stripes"* (Luke 12:47, 48).

If those standing in the pulpits of our land today do not know the truth, it is not God's fault. They have Bibles, they have been exposed to the true Gospel, they could KNOW the truth if they wanted to know it. Someone may say, "Preacher, the modernistic schools which they attend destroy their faith." A young man or woman who is born again has no business attending such a school! But the sad thing about the majority of liberal preachers who are coming off the seminary assembly lines in our modern institutions is that they had nothing to lose when they entered; they had never been saved in the first place! They took up the ministry as a lawyer takes up Law. True Bible ministers do not "choose a profession"; *they are called of God!* Read I Peter 2:6 and you will see that a God-called preacher is not driven about by every wind of doctrine.

Not only should the PREACHER be "salty" — with a Gospel that sweetens Christians and irritates hypocrites and Pharisees — but *every child of God should* be just as salty for Jesus as is the preacher! Someone has said, "I looked for the church — and I found it in the world; I looked for the world — and I found it in the church." There is more truth than poetry in that statement!

The most uncomfortable place on earth for a sinner is in the presence of consecrated Christians. The pure life of a child of God reproves the sinner of his or her impure life. The righteousness of God within God's child reproves the unrighteousness which abides in the heart and life of the sinner. The Christian and the sinner do not think the same thoughts, they do not speak the same language, they do not sing the same songs, they do not love the same things nor enjoy the same pleasures. Therefore, they clash; they are not at ease in each other's presence.

But in this "lovey-dovey, brotherhood-of-man, everybody is good, nobody is bad" age, there are not many church members who live such holy lives that the sinner is uncomfortable in their presence. Most sinners feel perfectly at ease at church parties, carnivals, church suppers and dances. Such religion is "GOOD FOR NOTHING" and should be "cast out and trodden under foot of men!"

Some will say that *fellowship* is the mark of the New Testament Christianity. I wonder what the Word of God means when it tells us: "Abstain from all appearance of evil" (I Thess. 5:22). " . . . Have no fellowship with the unfruitful works of darkness, but rather reprove them" (Eph. 5:11). Or, "Be ye not unequally yoked together with unbelievers: for what fellowship hath righteousness with unrighteousness? and what communion hath light with darkness? And what concord hath Christ with Belial? or what part hath he that believeth with an infidel? And what agreement hath the temple of God with idols? For ye are the temple of the living God; as God hath said, I will dwell in them, and walk in them; and I will be their God, and they shall be my people. *Wherefore come out from among them, and be ye separate, saith the Lord,* and touch not the unclean thing; and I will receive you, And will be a Father unto you, and ye shall be my sons and daughters, saith the Lord Almighty" (II Cor. 6:14-18).

These words are inspired of God. They say what they mean, and they mean what they say. I therefore refuse to fellowship with any man who attempts to put Jesus Christ on the level with other men, or who denies His virgin birth. I refuse to fellowship with any man who denies the *verbal inspiration* of the Word of God. Insofar as I am concerned, that man is an infidel. Yet some of our religious leaders today tell us that we are supposed to fellowship with modernists, liberals, those of all faiths, cults, "isms," or whatever.

New Testament Christianity teaches us to be good "separators," not *good mixers*. We are to have no fellowship with any person who denies any part of the doctrine taught by Jesus: *"If there come any unto you, and bring not this doctrine, receive him not into your house, neither bid him God speed: For he that biddeth him God speed is partaker of his evil deeds"* (II John 10, 11).

God's preachers have always been unpopular — and they always will be. "Woe unto you, when all men shall speak well of you!" (Luke 6:26). If there has ever been a time when we who know the Lord should live salty lives for Jesus — and rub it in — *it is now!* My daily prayer is that God will help me to be a living example of God's grace, and that those with whom I come in contact may know that I have been with Jesus!

Believers, "(We) are the salt of the earth: but if the salt have lost his savour . . . it is thenceforth good for nothing, but to be cast out, and to be trodden under foot of men." Am I a "salty" Christian? Or am I *"good for nothing"?* Ask yourself that solemn question. May God help us to be examples of His grace, and not a DISGRACE to the God whom we claim to love and serve!

Snares

SNARES

"Moreover, he must have a good report of them which are without; lest he fall into reproach **and the snare of the devil**" (I Tim. 3:7).

There are two things every child of God needs to remember: (1) He has a WISE Keeper; (2) he has a WILY enemy who is always seeking to entangle a believer in snares. In this message I would like to point out several snares of the devil.

1. **Pride:**

Pride was the snare into which the devil himself fell (and as a result was changed from "the shining one" to the loathsome one). Ezekiel 28: 10-15 gives a description of the king of Tyrus (which applies to Satan), and from these verses we learn that this magnificent creature was perfect in wisdom, perfect in beauty, every precious stone was his covering, and he was referred to as "the anointed cherub that covereth." He was the "high sheriff" of God's throne; he was next to the Trinity in position in God's great heaven. God gave him that position, and Ezekiel 28:15 says, "Thou wast perfect in thy ways from the day that thou wast created **till iniquity was found in thee!**"

PRIDE was **the iniquity** that was found in Lucifer. Isaiah 14:12-15 clearly sets forth the sin that caused his downfall. He was no longer willing to be subordinate to God, and therefore he attempted to overthrow God and take God's position. Since the Creator is greater than the created (and Lucifer was a created being), God threw him out of heaven, and he became the enemy of God and of every believer. In Luke 10:18 Jesus said, "I beheld Satan **as lightning** fall from heaven!"

Pride is a snare of the devil. "God resisteth the proud, but giveth grace to the humble." The sin of pride has many colors and shapes; it is not always seen in the same form;

93

but **"Pride goeth before destruction, and an haughty spirit before a fall"** (Prov. 16:18). Satan is the originator of pride, and pride is definitely one of his most useful snares.

It is strange to me that some who claim to be followers of the Lamb of God demonstrate so much ungodly pride in their daily living. We who are believers have but one thing of which to boast—and that is **the grace of God** that made us what we are! Paul said, "I am what I am by the grace of God," and **were it not for God's love, mercy and grace I would be roasting in hell today!** The closer we live to Jesus, the more we will lift HIM up and the less we will talk about ourselves. We are admonished to take up the cross with Jesus, get into the yoke with Him, and follow in His steps. May God deliver us from the snare of pride.

2. **Riches:**

". . . They that will be rich fall into temptation and a snare . . ." (I Tim. 6:9). The glitter of gold has fascinated many believers—to their overthrow and defeat as a witness for the Christ who saved them. The lure of gold and love of riches has been used of the devil to destroy many. The disciples were astonished when Jesus preached a sermon on riches:

"And Jesus looked round about, and saith unto His disciples, How hardly shall they that have riches enter into the kingdom of God! And the disciples were astonished at His words. But Jesus answereth again, and saith unto them, Children, how hard it is for them that trust in riches to enter into the kingdom of God! It is easier for a camel to go through the eye of a needle, than for a rich man to enter into the kingdom of God. And they were astonished out of measure, saying among themselves, Who then can be saved? And Jesus looking upon them saith, With men it is impossible, but not with God; for with God all things are possible" (Mark 10:23-27).

The Bible does not tell us that **money** is the root of all evil, but that "the LOVE of money is the root of all evil" (I Tim. 6:10). It is possible for a person to be rich and not **love** money, but such a one is rare indeed. I believe God calls some men to make money, and that He blesses those who do not allow money to become their god. A believer who will give unto the Lord that which is rightfully His, and then in addition to the tithe, **give gifts,** will be blessed of God and his earthly wealth will be multiplied; but if we rob God, He will withhold material blessings from us. If we sow sparingly, we shall **reap** sparingly; But if we sow bountifully, we shall reap bountifully. God loves a cheerful giver.

In Acts 5:1-9 we read the sad story of Ananias and Sapphira, his wife. The church in Jerusalem was really on fire for God. Believers were selling their possessions and giving the money to the church. For some reason not fully understandable, Ananias and Sapphira sold a possession and lied about it. Many Bible believers think these people were born again, and that they committed the sin unto death. Frankly, I do not know whether they were saved or not—but they wanted to stand in good with the church in Jerusalem, and so they sold their property—but they withheld part of the money. When they went into the temple and laid their money at the apostle's feet, their sin was pointed out by the Holy Spirit. Ananias dropped dead—and was buried without a funeral service . . . without a prayer, without a song, without flowers. A bit later his wife, Sapphira, came into the temple, and she agreed to the lie that her husband had told— she dropped dead and was buried in like manner as Ananias. The love of riches cost Ananias and Sapphira a tremendous price, and they are not the last to be caught in that snare.

Believer, do not allow the love of riches to rob you of your spiritual birthright; never allow it to fasten its fangs in your soul. The glitter of gold might lead you astray and cost you more in the end than it will provide as you travel life's journey. I am willing to use for God every dollar He places in my hands; but I do not want one dollar that cannot be used to His glory!

3. **Sleepiness** (laziness):

". . . And that they may recover themselves out of the snare of the devil, who are taken captive by him at his will" (II Tim. 2:26). The Greek reads, ". . . **Awake** themselves out of the snare of the devil."

In this verse, Paul is advising spiritual soldiers. In the opening verse of this chapter, he says, "Thou therefore, my son, be strong in the grace that is in Christ Jesus." Later in the same chapter he admonishes believers to study to show themselves approved unto God, workmen that need not be ashamed, rightly handling the Word of God. He tells us to shun "profane babblings"; but we are to increase in godliness; we are to purge ourselves and be a vessel of honor—sanctified, set apart, and dedicated for the Master's use, prepared at all times to do every good work.

Believers are to flee lust. We are to follow righteousness, faith, charity, peace and godliness. Foolish and unlearned questions we are to avoid, for these things gender strife. The servant of the Lord must not strive, but must be gentle to all men, ready to teach at all times, patient, instructing those who do not know God, or who are not spiritually minded. In so doing, we will remain alert and not fall into the snare of sleeping when we should be on the job for Jesus.

To the believers in Rome, Paul said, ". . . Knowing the time, that now it is high time to awake out of sleep: for now is our salvation nearer than when we believed. The night is far spent, the day is at hand: let us therefore cast off the works of darkness, and let us put on the armour of light. Let us walk honestly, as in the day; not in rioting and drunkenness, not in chambering and wantonness, not in strife and envying" (Rom. 13:11-13).

Believers should be sober and alert at all times, because the devil—either as a roaring lion or as an angel of light—is always on the alert to place a snare in our path. If he cannot damn a soul and send a person to hell, his next move is to cause that believer to became a slothful, asleep-on-the-job Christian. We are to occupy until Jesus comes. We should buy up every opportunity to point weary souls to the Lamb of God. May God help us as believers to be alert at all times for Jesus.

4. Idolatry:

"And Gideon made an ephod . . . WHICH THING BE-CAME A SNARE unto Gideon, and to his house" (Judges 8:27). Idolatry is committed when anything or anyone takes the place of God in our life. God **must** occupy first place in all that we are and in all that we do if we hope to receive His blessings. To put **anything** above God in our thinking, living, planning—or in love—is to become an idolater. This is a snare used by the devil to trap and damn the sinner, and to rob the believer of his spiritual birthright of joy unspeakble and full of glory, with a full reward at the end of life's journey!

Many times idolatry slips into a believer's life through things that seem harmless and insignificant. Sometimes a mother idolizes her children; when the babies come along she spends all of her time thinking of and planning for them. She stops attending church and prayer meeting, and devotes her entire attention to the children and the home. This is not right. We should not allow anything or anybody to come between us and our duty to God—Bible reading, prayer, attending church. If a normal, healthy baby stands in the way of a mother attending church, **God can remove the baby** so that there will be no hindrance! Sometimes God removes a husband, a wife, a mother or a father who

97

has become the idol of loved ones—a position that only God should hold.

Do not allow your business, your home, your friends, your loved ones, your money to stand between you and your duty to God, for such is the snare of idolatry. I John is one of the most precious books in the Bible—especially for the believer. It is God's love-letter to His little children, and it closes with these words: "LITTLE CHILDREN, KEEP YOURSELVES FROM IDOLS." Yes, it is possible for God's dear children to have idols.

That does not mean that a born again child of God will go to hell, but it does mean that the devil uses the snare of idolatry to rob the believer of his spiritual birthright. Do not let it happen to you! "Look to yourselves, that we lose not those things which we have wrought, **but that we receive a full reward**" (II John 8). This has nothing to do with losing the soul, but losing our reward ("the things which WE have wrought").

If a believer allows the snares of pride, riches, sleepiness, or idolatry to come between him and God, he will lose part, if not all, of his reward.

This truth is clearly set forth and outlined in I Corinthians 3:11-15. God deliver us from the snare of idolatry. My prayer is, that I may make the things of God the idol of my every thought and action. Whether I eat or drink or whatsoever I do, my desire is to do it all to the glory of God.

5. **Fear:**

"The fear of man bringeth a snare" (Prov. 29:25). The believer is to fear none save God—and if we fear God, we need fear nought else. God is Almighty, all-sufficient—and "If God be for us, who can be against us?" (Rom. 8:31). "FEAR NOT; I am the first and the last: I am He that liveth, and was dead; and, behold, I am alive for evermore, Amen; and have the keys of hell and of death" (Rev. 1:17b, 18).

Jesus said, "Fear them not therefore: for there is nothing covered, that shall not be revealed; and hid, that shall not be known . . . and fear not them which kill the body, but are not able to kill the soul: but rather fear him which is able to destroy both soul and body in hell" (Matt. 10:26, 28).

The snare of fear has sent many a soul to hell! A lengthy sermon could be delivered on that subject. Many have desired to become Christians—**but they have been afraid of what their loved ones, friends, or neighbors might do.** They have **feared they will lose their social position, or their job, or the respect of neighbors, friends, or relatives. They are afraid of what people will say if they cease to partake of this lust or that pleasure.** The fear of man is definitely a snare, and if we fear man rather than God, then the end for us is hell.

The snare of fear has robbed many Christians of their spiritual birthright. In the Book of Acts we read of disciples who were fearless. They were "dare-saints." Even after they were dragged into the council halls and threatened, they went back to the same streets to preach Jesus Christ— crucified, buried and risen! They did not fear the rulers— they feared only God and were determined to proclaim the whole Gospel.

Fear of man has caused many a minister to deviate from preaching pure, full Gospel, lest he lose his church or some influential member might leave the church because of the boldness of the preacher in naming sin and preaching against worldliness and ungodliness. If the minister preaches the doctrine **bidden by Jesus to be preached,** he can rest assured that he will not be well spoken of by all men; but every minister and every believer should know, "Beware of him of whom all men speak well."

I John 4:17-19 is an enlightening passage concerning fear: "Herein is our love made perfect, that we may have boldness in the day of judgment: because as He is, so are we in this world. There is no fear in love; but perfect love casteth out fear: because fear hath torment. He that feareth is not made perfect in love. We love Him, because He first loved us."

If we are truly born again there is no reason to fear the past, the present nor the future. There is no reason for us to be afraid to live, nor afraid to die. There is no reason why we should be afraid to face man, or face God. Jesus Christ is the all-sufficient One—He saves, He keeps, He delivers, and He will stand to confess us before the Father in that last day of the judgment. If we know that we are truly born again, we know that He who loved us so much that He shed His blood for the remission of sin, will keep and direct us, and will stand with us to say to the heavenly Father, "This is my child." The Father will then say, "Enter thou into the joys of thy Lord." Perfect love casteth out fear! If you are afraid to die, if you are afraid to meet God, if you are afraid to face the future, then, dear friend, get alone on your knees in your prayer closet and check up! It could be that the devil slipped you a counterfeit.

6. The last snare we will mention is **evil companionship:** "They shall be snares and traps unto you " (Josh. 23:13 in part).

If we walk with the world, our spiritual life will become tarnished. If we are friends with the world, we are enemies to God. We are commanded, "Come ye out from among them . . . and touch not the unclean." Paul admonishes the believers in Thessalonica to "Abstain from all appearance of evil." John commands, "Love not the world, neither the things that are in the world. If any man love the world, the love of the Father is not in him. For all that is in the world, the lust of the flesh, and the lust of the eyes, and the pride of life, is not of the Father, but is of the world. And the world passeth away, and the lust thereof; but he that doeth the will of God abideth for ever" (I John 2:15-17). The children of God must not love this present world. The lighter we cling to things of the world, the tighter our grip on heaven. All that is in this world—the lust of the flesh, the lust of the eye, the pride of life—will lead us FROM God, not TO Him. The love of the world and the evil IN the world are snares. How can two walk together except they be agreed? We cannot walk with the world unless we compromise our spiritual convictions.

The believer is IN the world, but not OF the world. They that are in the flesh cannot please God, "But ye are not in the flesh, but in the Spirit" (Rom. 8:9). Every born again believer possesses the Holy Spirit to direct and lead him. David said, "He leadeth me in the paths of righteousness for His name's sake." Therefore the believer who falters and fails in spiritual matters, taking God's second or third best for his life, has no one to blame but himself. "For we have not an high priest which cannot be touched with the feeling of our infirmities; but was in all points tempted like as we are, yet without sin" (Heb. 4:15).

I close this message with the same statement as that with which I opened it: There are two things every believer needs to remember: (1) We have a WISE Keeper—the Lord Jesus, our Mediator (I Tim. 2:5), our High Priest (Heb. 4:15), our Deliverer (I Cor. 10:13, Rom. 8:35-39).

(2) We need to remember our WILY enemy—the devil. He will never cease to tempt and try to lead us astray. He will never cease to place snares in our path; but we can be "more than conquerors through Him that loved us" (Rom. 8:37).

Be alert—and be aware that pride is a snare of the devil. The love of riches can very well be used of Satan to lead us astray; riches can become an idol. Be alert to the snare of sleepiness or laziness, the snare of idolatry, the snare of fear, and the snare of evil companionship. God help us as believers to remember that although the devil cannot damn us, he will never cease to attempt to lead us astray **as believers**, and cause us to be unfruitful and unprofitable servants of God. Whether therefore we eat or drink, or whatsoever we do as a believer, let us do all TO THE GLORY OF GOD!

The Word Became Flesh

THE WORD BECAME FLESH

John's Gospel is the "salvation Gospel." John was truly a seer — he recognized and recorded what others seemingly failed to see. It was John who recognized the Lord on the morning He had breakfast prepared for the weary disciples who had fished all night and had taken no fish. The other disciples did not recognize Jesus as He stood on the shore and watched the little ship approach land; but John knew who He was: "Therefore **that disciple whom Jesus loved** saith unto Peter, It is the Lord!" (John 21:7).

It was also John the Beloved who said, ". . . Many other signs truly did Jesus in the presence of His disciples, which are not written in this book: **But these are written, that ye might believe that Jesus is the Christ, the Son of God; and that believing, ye might have life through His name**" (John 20:30, 31).

These verses are the key to the Gospel of John; and in this marvelous Gospel we find a depth of thought that cannot be found in any of the other Gospels nor in any other book in the sacred library which comprises our Bible.

THE WORD

In the opening verse of John's Gospel we read, "In the beginning was the Word, and the Word was with God, and the Word was God." None of the other writers give this name to the Lord Jesus Christ. John recognized that the function of a word is to express the mind and heart of the one speaking. Without words, the mind of man could not be known; and if God had not expressed Himself in The WORD, it would have been impossible for man to know God.

Paul describes it thus: "God, who at sundry times and in divers manners spake in time past unto the fathers by the prophets, hath in these last days spoken unto us by His Son, whom He hath appointed heir of all things, by whom also He made the worlds" (Heb. 1:1, 2).

"**From everlasting to everlasting,** thou art God!" (Psalm 90:1, 2). I readily confess that it is impossible for me to comprehend a God who has always been . . . but it is not not impossible for me to understand and believe that a Man named Jesus came into the world in a body 1900 years ago. He lived, walked and talked with men upon this earth. He died, was buried, rose again and ascended back to the Father. I do not fully understand the Incarnation; I do not fully understand the bodily resurrection: but I believe that Jesus lived, died, and rose again. It is beyond my ability to think in terms of a God who is a Spirit (John 4:24), a God who had no beginning, a God who has always been and always will be. "In The beginning was the WORD, and the WORD was with God, and the WORD was God . . . and **the WORD was made flesh . . ."** (John 1:1 and 14).

Jesus was the Word in flesh. What the Law could not do, Jesus did in flesh (Rom 8:2-4). In the first Epistle of John we read, "That which was from the beginning, which we have heard, which we have seen with our eyes, which we have looked upon, and our hands have handled, of the Word of life; (For the life was manifested, and we have seen it, and bear witness, and shew unto you that eternal life, which was with the Father, and was manifested unto us;) That which we have seen and heard declare we unto you, that ye also may have fellowship with us: and truly our fellowship is with the Father, and with His Son Jesus Christ. And these things write we unto you, that your joy may be full. This then is the message which we have heard of Him, and declared unto you, that God is light, and in Him is no darkness at all. If we say that we have fellowship with Him, and walk in darkness, we lie, and do not the truth: But if we walk in the light, as He is in the light, we have fellowship one with another, and the blood of Jesus Christ His Son cleanseth us from all sin" (I John 1:1-7).

John testified, "That **which was** from the beginning (in

the beginning **was the Word)** ¯which we have **heard** . . . which we have **seen** . . . which our hands have **handled,** of the **WORD of life** . . . for the life was manifested . . ." (I John 1:1 ff). God is the author of ALL life. He created Adam from the dust of the ground, and Adams was only a dust-man until God breathed into his nostrils the breath of life. The **life of God** was manifested in the flesh in which Jesus lived upon this earth for thirty-three and one-half years. In II Corinthians 5:19 we are plainly told that **Jesus was GOD in flesh.** Therefore, the Word that was "in the beginning" was wrapped up in flesh and brought down to man in the Person of the Lord Jesus Christ.

We will never fully understand nor properly appreciate the importance of God's Word as long as we remain in this body of flesh; but we do know the devil has done his best to discredit and destroy the Word — and no wonder:

"Verily, verily, I say unto you, **He that heareth my Word; and believeth on Him that sent me, hath everlasting life,** and shall not come into condemnation; but is passed from death unto life" (John 5:24).

It is impossible to be saved apart from hearing the Word. The Word tells us that God so loved the world that He gave Jesus to die on the cross for us. The Word makes clear to us the truth that Jesus willingly laid His life down that we might have life. The Word tells us, "Come unto me, all ye that labour and are heavy laden, and I will give you rest . . . Come unto me and I will in no wise cast you out! Let him that is thirsty come, and drink of the water of life freely." We would never have known these wonderful truths had it not been for the Word — but let us go a step further:

In Ephesians 2:8, 9 we read, "For by grace are ye saved through faith; and that not of yourselves: it is the gift of God: not of works, lest any man should boast." We are saved by God's grace — but saving grace becomes ours only by faith. Where do we get the faith to **appropriate** the grace of God? We could not know the answer to that question were it not for the Word of God: "So then **faith cometh by hearing, and hearing by the Word of God**" (Rom. 10:17). We are saved by God's grace — **through faith;** and faith to appropriate the grace of God comes only **by hearing the Word of God.** No wonder the devil tries to keep ministers from preaching the pure Word of God! The Word brings the knowledge of God's love, and it is the Word that implants faith in our hearts — faith to trust in the finished work and the shed blood of Jesus for salvaton. But shall we go a step further?

We are saved by God's grace — but saving grace becomes ours only by faith. After we become a child of God, how do we **keep** this salvation? How do we **live** the salvation which we receive through the grace of God by faith in His finished work? Again the answer is found in the Word of God:

"Whosoever believeth that Jesus is the Christ is born of God: and every one that loveth Him that begat loveth him also that is begotten of Him. By this we know that we love the children of God, when we love God, and keep His commandments. For this is the love of God, that we keep His commandments: and His commandments are not grievous. For whatsoever is born of God overcometh the world: and this is the victory that overcometh the world, even our faith. Who is he that overcometh the world, but he that believeth that Jesus is the Son of God?" (I John 5:1-5).

These verses tell us that whosoever believes that Jesus is the Christ **is born of God.** But how could we ever have believed that Jesus IS the Christ were it not for the Word? Whosoever is born of God overcomes the world — "and this is the victory that overcometh the world, **even our faith.**" But faith to overcome the world, like faith to be saved, comes by hearing the Word of God. The only way anyone can ever have faith that will bring either salvation OR victory is to hear the Word of God. It is impossible to do business with Almighty God except through faith. "He that cometh to God **must believe that He is,** and that He is a rewarder of them that diligently seek Him" (Heb. 11:6 b). No person can be saved unless he believes the record God has given of His Son:

"For there are three that bear record in heaven, the Father, the Word, and the Holy Ghost: and these three are one . . . If we receive the witness of men, the witness of God is greater: for this is the witness of God which He hath testified of His Son. He that believeth on the Son of God hath the witness in himself: he that believeth not God hath made Him a liar; because he believeth not the record that God gave of His Son. **And this is the record, that God hath given to us eternal life, and this life is in His Son.** He that hath the Son hath life; and he that hath not the Son of God hath not life. These things have I written unto you that believe on the name of the Son of God; that ye may know that ye have eternal life, and that ye may believe on the name of the Son of God" (I John 5:7, 9-13).

Eternal life is in God's Son, the Lord Jesus Christ: "And the Word was made flesh, and dwelt among us, (and we beheld His glory, the glory as of the only begotten of the Father,) full of grace and truth" (John 1:14).

"Ye shall know the truth, and the truth shall make you free" (John 8:32).

"If the Son therefore shall make you free, ye shall be free indeed" (John 8:36).

"As many as received Him, to them gave He power to become the sons of God, even to them that believe on His name: which were born, not of blood, nor of the will of the flesh, nor of the will of man, but of God" (John 1:12, 13).

If there is any one thing that is crystal clear in the Word of God it is that we are saved by hearing the Word. The Word is the incorruptible seed that brings eternal life

109

through the new birth (I Pet. 1:23).

We are saved by grace through faith (Eph. 2:8). We overcome the world by faith (I John 5:2-5). The just shall live by faith (Rom. 1:17); and "whatsoever is not of faith is sin" (Rom. 14:23).

THE LIGHT

In this tremendous salvation Gospel we read: "There was a man sent from God, whose name was John. The same came for a witness, to bear witness of the Light, that all men through Him might believe. He was not that Light, but was sent to bear witness of that Light. That was the true Light, which lighteth every man that cometh into the world" (John 1:6-9).

John the Baptist readily admitted that he was not "that Light," but that he was sent **to bear witness** of that Light . . . "which was the true Light which lighteth every man that cometh into the world," telling us that man had strayed far, far from God and had lost his way in the darkness of sin; but the coming of the Man Christ Jesus (the Word in flesh) meant that now a Light was shining — THE Light that would point poor, lost, wandering sinners back to God. Jesus was the true Light, and without His guiding beam man would remain lost eternally. "But if we walk in the light, as He is in the light, we have fellowship one with another, and the blood of Jesus Christ His Son cleanseth us from all sin" (I John 1:7).

Jesus said, "I am the light of the world: he that followeth me shall not walk in darkness, but shall have the light of life" (John 8:12). Since Jesus came, there is no longer any excuse for men to grope in darkness: "And this is the condemnation, THAT LIGHT IS COME INTO THE WORLD, and men loved darkness rather than light, because their deeds were evil. For every one that doeth evil hateth the light, neither cometh to the light, lest his deeds should be reproved. But he that doeth truth cometh to the light, that his deeds may be made manifest, that they are wrought in God" (John 3:19-21).

Men are lost today because they refuse to come to the Light. All are invited — "whosoever will" can come to the Light if they are willing. Matthew 4:16, 17 tells us, "The people which sat in darkness saw great light; and to them which sat in the region and shadow of death light is sprung up. From that time Jesus began to preach, and to say, Repent: for the kingdom of heaven is at hand."

Not only is Jesus **salvation** — He is also the Light that points us TO the way of salvation. "Thomas saith unto Him, Lord, we know not whither thou goest; and how can we know the way? Jesus saith unto him, **I am the way, the truth, and the life: no man cometh unto the Father, but by me**" (John 14:5, 6).

THE CHRIST

I suppose there has been no mortal on the face of this earth who could have been more proud — and rightly so — than John the Baptist; but John was very careful to point all honor, glory, praise and worship to the Word in flesh, the true Light — the Christ:

"John bare witness of Him, and cried, saying, This was He of whom I spake, He that cometh after me is preferred before me: for He was before me. And of His fullness have all we received, and grace for grace. For the law was given by Moses, but grace and truth came by Jesus Christ. No man hath seen God at any time; the only begotten Son, which is in the bosom of the Father, He hath declared Him. And this is the record of John, when the Jews sent priests and Levites from Jerusalem to ask him, Who art thou? And he confessed, and denied not; but confessed, I am not the Christ. And they asked him, What then? Art thou Elias? And he saith, I am not. Art thou that prophet? And he answered, No. Then said they unto him, Who are thou? that we may give an answer to them that sent us. What

111

sayest thou of thyself? He said, I am the voice of one crying in the wilderness, Make straight the way of the Lord, as said the prophet Esaias" (John 1:15-23).

Of course the religionists could not understand such words as "He that cometh after me is preferred before me, for **He was** before me." John the Baptist knew that he was announcing the Messiah, the Lamb of God, the King. And he testified that the true Light was the One who had brought grace and truth down to man: **"No man hath seen God at any time** . . . the only begotten Son which is in the bosom of the Father, He hath declared Him."

Jesus came into the world to declare God's love, to demonstrate God's love, to live God's love, tenderness, and compassion in everything He did and said. He came not to do His own will, but to do the will of the Father. Just before He died He lifted His eyes to heaven and announced in prayer, "I have finished the work thou gavest me to do" (John 17:1-4). John the Baptist wanted all eyes on Jesus. He did not want anyone to misunderstand his message. He pointed to the Christ, not to himself.

THE LAMB

And then one day John announced, **"Behold the Lamb of God, which taketh away the sin of the world!"** (John 1:29).

What a tremendous declaration! John knew that in the Old Testament era the lambs offered by the worshippers, the blood shed by the priest, covered only the sins of the individual — and **that** only for a season, because the offerings must be repeated again and again and again. But John announced the Lamb that would take away — not only the **sin of the individual,** but the sin of the **whole world!**

In I John 2:1, 2 we read, "My little children, these things write I unto you, that ye sin not. And if any man sin, we have an advocate with the Father, Jesus Christ the righteous; and He is the propitiation for our sins: and not for our's only, but also for the sins of the world." It is clear that Jesus' blood was shed for the remission of sin — not only for the individual sinner, but for the sin that would damn all men.

In this day there are many who teach that is is not necessary to believe in a blood-religion. They call us "slaughterhouse preachers," and say that we preach a butcher-house Gospel; but I remind all who deny the blood that **"without shedding of blood is no remission"** (Heb. 9:22).

Again: "Blessed be the God and Father of our Lord Jesus Christ, who hath blessed us with all spiritual blessings in heavenly places in Christ: According as He hath chosen us in Him before the foundation of the world, that we should be holy and without blame before Him in love: Having predestinated us unto the adoption of children by Jesus Christ to Himself, according to the good pleasure of His will, to the praise of the glory of His grace, wherein He hath made us accepted in the beloved. In whom we have redemption through His blood, the forgiveness of sins, according to the riches of His grace" (Eph. 1:3-7).

Redemption is found only through His precious blood. The forgiveness of sins is found **only through His precious blood**. It is the blood that cleanses from all sin (I John 1:7). "And from Jesus Christ, who is the faithful witness, and the first begotten of the dead, and the prince of the kings of the earth. Unto him that loved us, and washed us from our sins in His own blood!" (Rev. 1:5).

> "There is a fountain filled with blood
> Drawn from Immanuel's veins
> And sinners, plunged beneath that flood,
> Lose all their guilty stains."

May I ask you, dear reader, Are **you** washed in the blood? If you are not, you are lost. There is no salvation, no redemption, and no forgiveness apart from the shed blood of the Lord Jesus Christ. If you are not sure that your sins are covered by His blood, bow your head this moment and behold the Lamb of God, slain for the remission of sin!

I Peter 1:18-25: "Forasmuch as ye know that ye were not redeemed with corruptible things, as silver and gold, from your vain conversation received by tradition from your fathers; But with the precious blood of Christ, as of a lamb without blemish and without spot: who verily was fore-ordained before the foundation of the world, but was manifest in these last times for you. Who by Him do believe in God, that raised Him up from the dead, and gave Him glory; that your faith and hope might be in God. Seeing that ye have purified your souls in obeying the truth through the Spirit unto unfeigned love of the brethren, see that ye love one another with a pure heart fervently: Being born again, not of corruptible seed, but of incorruptible, by the word of God, which liveth and abideth for ever. For all flesh is as grass, and all the glory of man as the flower of grass. The grass withereth, and the flower thereof falleth away: But the word of the Lord endureth for ever. And this is the word which by the Gospel is preached unto you." That settles it!

THE SON

In this majestic mountain-peak of holy Scripture, John announces the Word, the Light, the Christ, the Lamb — and now he points to **the Son:** "And I saw, and bare record, **that this is the Son of God**" (John 1:34).

There is not one word in all the Bible that was put there for the purpose of filling space or closing a gap. Every name given to the Lord Jesus Christ is significant. The name "Son" was not given to Him to indicate that He was inferior to the Father. There are instances when a son is even greater than his father; but this is not true of Jesus. He said, **"I and my Father are one"** (John 10:30). John points out "the Son" here to indicate that this Personality

114

of whom he speaks is very God — in essence and in nature. He is not just a man, nor just a great preacher; but He is God's Son . . . He is the WORD that became flesh.

Salvation is in the Son: "Christ in you, the hope of glory" (Col. 1:27). "There is therefore now no condemnation to them which are in Christ Jesus" (Rom. 8:1). "Ye are dead, and your life is hid with Christ in God" (Col. 3:3). "He that hath the Son hath life; and he that hath not the Son of God hath not life" (I John 5:12). "He that believeth on the Son hath everlasting life: and he that believeth not the Son shall not see life; but the wrath of God abideth on him" (John 3:36). "IF THE SON therefore shall make you free, ye shall be free indeed" (John 8:36).

When John the Baptist baptized Jesus, God the Father announced in an audible voice, **"THIS IS MY BELOVED SON, IN WHOM I AM WELL PLEASED"** (Matt. 3:17). Again God the Father put His stamp of approval upon the Man, Christ Jesus, by saying, "THIS IS MY BELOVED SON, IN WHOM I AM WELL PLEASED; HEAR YE HIM" (Matt. 17:5b).

The enemies of Jesus said, ". . . He ought to die, because He made Himself the Son of God" (John 19:7); but this was a false accusation. Jesus did not need to announce that He was God's Son. **God** announced it — at His birth, at His baptism, on the Mount of Transfiguration, and on other occasions in various ways. He IS the Son of God, **very God;** and dear reader, where you spend eternity will be determined by your answer to the question, **"What think ye of** Christ? Whose Son is He?" (Matt. 22:42).

THE MASTER

"Again the next day after John stood, and two of his disciples; and looking upon Jesus as He walked, he saith, Behold the Lamb of God! And the two disciples heard him speak, and they followed Jesus. Then Jesus turned, and saw them following, and saith unto them, What seek ye?

They said unto Him, Rabbi, (which is to say, being interpreted, Master,) where dwellest thou? He saith unto them, Come and see. They came and saw where He dwelt, and abode with Him that day: for it was about the tenth hour. One of the two which heard John speak, and followed Him, was Andrew, Simon Peter's brother. He first findeth his own brother Simon, and saith unto him, We have found the Messias, which is, being interpreted, the Christ" (John 1:35-41).

Two of John's disciples went home with Jesus that day, and spent the rest of the day with Him. Andrew never got over it: he became the prince of soul-winners. It was Andrew who searched for food to feed the hungry multitude, and who found the boy with the loaves and fishes, while the others were lamenting the fact that they did not have enough money to buy bread sufficient "that every one of them may take a little."

It was to Andrew that Philip brought the Greeks who desired to see Jesus. Andrew did not know the answer, but he knew the One who knows ALL things; and he brought the Greeks to Jesus.

We do not know what Jesus talked about during the hours the two disciples spent with Him where He lived, but whatever He said, whatever He taught captivated their lives and they became fishers of men.

The keynote of the ministry of Jesus while here upon this earth was, "Come unto me, all ye that labour and are heavy laden, and I will give you rest . . . Him that cometh to me, I will in no wise cast out" (Matt. 11:28; John 6:37). Any time, anywhere any person asks Jesus "Where dwellest thou?" He will always invite, "Come and see!" And any person who will sincerely allow the Lord Jesus to visit with him, any person who will read the Gospels with an open mind and an open heart, will be captivated by the message and fall in love with **The Word.**

THE KING

John could not close this glorious chapter without pointing to the King of kings and Lord of lords. Philip had become a soul-winner: "Now Philip was of Bethsaida, the city of Andrew and Peter. Philip findeth Nathanael, and saith unto him, We have found Him, of whom Moses in the law, and the prophets did write, Jesus of Nazareth, the son of Joseph." Nathanael was skeptical. He asked Philip, "Can there any good thing come out of Nazareth? Philip saith unto him, Come and see!" (John 1:44-46).

Philip could have started a real religious argument here — but he was too wise to allow the devil to cause him to lose the opportunity to win Nathanael to the Messiah. He did not argue as to whether or not any good thing could come out of Nazareth; he used the words of the Master Soul-Winner: **"Come and see!"** Philip believed in his heart that if he could only get Nathanael in touch with Jesus, when he met the Messiah he would fall in love with Him. He knew that was what had happened to **him,** and he believed the same thing would happen to Nathanael. When Nathanael saw the Lord Jesus Christ he was convinced:

"Jesus saw Nathanael coming to Him, and saith of him, Behold an Israelite indeed, in whom is no guile! Nathanael saith unto Him, Whence knowest thou me? Jesus answered and said unto him, Before that Philip called thee, when thou wast under the fig tree, I saw thee. Nathanael answered and said unto Him, Rabbi, thou art the Son of God; thou art the King of Israel. Jesus answered and said unto him, because I said unto thee, I saw thee under the fig tree, believest thou? thou shalt see greater things than these" (John 1:47-50).

Yes, Nathanael confessed with his mouth, he believed in his heart, and he became a true disciple of Jesus Christ (Rom. 10:9, 10). But Nathanael went a step further; He not only confessed Jesus as Rabbi, the Son of God, but he announced, **"Thou Art the King of Israel!"** Nathanael had crowned the Messiah King of his life, and even though he might not have fully understood what he said, through the power of the Holy Ghost he announced that this Messiah with whom he had fallen in love would one day be King of a kingdom — King of kings and Lord of lords! That was a great day for Nathanael.

I say, unsaved friend, in the words of Philip, "Come and see!" You have heard much about Jesus; you have heard many things about Christianity; you have heard much about religion, churches, and preachers. But the best way to find out what **Jesus** is, what Jesus does — and what He can do for **you** — is simply to "Come — and SEE!"

I accepted that same invitation more than twenty-nine years ago, and I can testify today that He is more than I ever fancied He could be! He's the fairest of ten thousand to my soul. Dear friend, if you are not a born again child of God, if you are not saved by grace, let me invite you right now, Come to Jesus by faith, and **see for yourself** what He will do in your heart and in your life!

THE SON OF MAN

"And He saith unto him, Verily, verily, I say unto you, Hereafter ye shall see heaven open, and the angels of God ascending and descending upon the Son of man" (John 1:51).

Certainly the words "Son of man" are a fitting climax to the masterly introduction to the salvation Gospel. What words with which to end this chapter! Jesus was the Word in flesh, very God in flesh. He did not blush to say, "I and my Father are one"; nor to say, "Philip, if you have seen me, you have seen the Father; for I am in the Father and the Father in me." He was **the Word** in flesh; He was the true **Light**; He was **the Christ of God** — the Christ who was in the bosom of God, but who took a body and in that body brought God down to man. He was **the Lamb of God,**

118

without spot, without wrinkle, without blemish. He was **the Son of God,** virgin-born. He was the **Master** of all teachers, and He was **born to be King of Israel.** One day He will sit on the throne of David and reign over the house of Jacob.

But He was also **the Son of man.** Jesus was the God-man — He was God, and He was man. He was deity in flesh, and what the law could not do because of the weakness of the flesh, God did in Jesus, made **like unto** sinful flesh. Thank God, Jesus walked upon this earth in a body like unto our bodies, tempted in all points as we are — yet without sin. In that body He overcame the world, the flesh, and the devil. He suffered, bled, and died — and in that body He satisfied every demand of God's holiness, God's Law; and when He literally laid His life down and gave His Spirit back to the Father, He said, **"It is finished!"** And now God can be just, and yet through the shed blood of Jesus Christ, can justify the ungodly:

"But now the righteousness of God without the Law is manifested . . . being justified freely by His grace through the redemption that is in Christ Jesus; Whom God hath set forth to be a propitiation through faith in His blood, to declare His righteousness for the remission of sins that are past, through the forbearance of God; to declare, I say, at this time His righteousness; THAT HE MIGHT BE JUST, AND THE JUSTIFIER OF HIM WHICH BELIEVETH IN JESUS . . . Therefore we conclude that a man is justified by faith without the deeds of the law" (Rom. 3:21, 24-26, 28).

I would like to say with Paul, "Thanks be unto God for His unspeakable gift" (II Cor. 9:15). The **birth** of Jesus was contrary to the laws of life. The **death** of Jesus was contrary to the laws of death. The Lord Jesus Christ never planted a grain of corn, He did not own a fishing boat; but He could feed five thousand and have a heaping basket left over for each of the twelve disciples. He did not own a beautiful home with carpets and lovely furnishings; but He walked on such a carpet as none other ever walked upon: He walked upon the waters of the Sea of Galilee! His earthly ministry was short — He preached for only three years. He wrote no commentaries on the Gospel — He WAS the Gospel! He built no churches — He is the head and the foundation OF The Church. He received no offerings; He had no monetary backing — yet He preached more sermons and blessed more people than any other living person, even though He did not have finances nor the support of things that money can buy.

Now, **after nineteen hundred years,** Jesus is the central character of human history. He is loved and worshipped by millions. He bears the burdens of tens of millions. **This Jesus:** Was He, as some suggest, the son of a blonde German soldier? Was He the son of Joseph and Mary? Did human blood pulse through His veins? Was the blood He shed on Calvary just ordinary blood? Let others believe what they may; but as for ME, I cry out, "NO! A million times no! MY LORD AND MY GOD was God's Christ, who died on a cross for the sins of the world!"

In His own precious words I close this message: "Verily, verily, I say unto you, He that heareth my word, and believeth on Him that sent me, hath everlasting life, and shall not come into condemnation; but is passed from death unto life" (John 5:24).

All anyone need do to be lost and eternally damned is to refuse to believe the record that God gives of His only begotten Son.

How Shall We Escape?

HOW SHALL WE ESCAPE?

"Therefore we ought to give the more earnest heed to the things which we have heard, lest at any time we should let them slip. For if the word spoken by angels was stedfast, and every transgression and disobedience received a just recompence of reward; how shall we escape, if we neglect so great salvation; which at the first began to be spoken by the Lord, and was confirmed unto us by them that heard Him; God also bearing them witness, both with signs and wonders, and with divers miracles, and gifts of the Holy Ghost, according to His own will?" (Hebrews 2:1-4).

The text: **"How shall we escape if we neglect so great salvation?"**

This "great salvation" about which we are to study in this message, is great in three ways. We will discuss these three great things about our salvation.

1. Our salvation is **great in its cost.**

I am wondering if someone is not saying, "Mr. Greene, have not I heard you and many other preachers make the statement that all one need do to be saved is to receive the finished work of Jesus? Have you not many times said on the radio, "Bow your head, confess your sins, call on the name of Jesus . . . and He will save you"?

I am guilty — I plead guilty to that charge; and if Jesus lets me live and He tarries, you will hear me say that ten thousand times more . . . on the radio, in the tent meetings, in churches and in my printed sermons. All any poor sinner can do to be saved is to receive the finished work of the Lord Jesus. Salvation is a gift, and "Whosoever shall call upon the name of the Lord shall be saved!" (Romans 10:13).

Perhaps someone is saying, "What is great about **that?**" Dear friend, it cost God the brightest Jewel in Heaven to make possible our salvation. "God so loved the world, that He gave His only begotten Son, that whosoever believeth in Him should not perish, but have everlasting life" (John 3:16).

"God commendeth His love toward us, in that, while we were yet sinners, Christ died for us" (Romans 5:8). God loved us while we were yet unlovely. God gave His Son to die for His enemies. "For scarcely for a righteous man will one die: yet peradventure for a good man some would even dare to die. But God commended His love toward us, in that, while we were yet sinners, Christ died for us" (Romans 5:7-8).

I repeat: It cost God His only begotten Son to make possible our salvation.

It cost Heaven the most precious Jewel there. Surely the angels must have bowed their heads. Surely the Cherubims must have folded their wings, surely Heaven went into mourning when it was announced that The Son, the Pearl of Great Price, would leave Heaven's glory and in one gigantic step would come to earth's sorrow to lay His life down for sinners!

That leads me to say it not only cost God His only Son, and cost Heaven the most precious Jewel there, but it cost The Son every drop of His precious blood, to make possible our salvation. Every pain He suffered — soul, spirit and body — every tear He shed, every heartache He endured, every miracle He performed, every good deed He did, every step He walked on this earth, every lash they put on His back, the crown of thorns He wore on His head, the scourging, the mocking, the spittle in His face, the plucking off of the hair from His cheeks, the spikes in His feet, the terrible cry of agony "My God, My God, why hast Thou forsaken Me?" . . . all these things were necessary that we might be able to call upon the name of the Lord and be saved.

If Jesus had not prayed, "Father, if it be possible let this cup pass from Me — nevertheless, not as I will but as Thou wilt," He could never have said, "It is finished!" And if He had never said "It is finished," we could have never called upon His name and found salvation. So let me hasten to say that the most expensive thing in Heaven or earth or under the earth, the most expensive thing known to God or the angels, (or to all creation), the most valuable thing ever known is **our salvation.** We are purchased at the tremendous price of His shed blood. We are redeemed through the power of His shed blood. We are kept because He suffered, died, was buried, and rose again. Because He lives, **we** live. Because He conquered, **we** conquer. Because He paid the debt, **we go free.** In Jesus Christ there is redemption:"But of Him are ye in Christ Jesus, who of God is made unto us wisdom, and righteousness, and sanctification, and redemption: That, according as it is written, he that glorieth, let Him glory in the Lord" (I Cor. 1:30-31).

Christ is made unto us wisdom . . . the wisdom through which we call. Christ is made unto us righteousness . . . He who knew no sin was made sin for us that we in Him might become righteous (II Cor. 5:21). Christ is made unto us sanctification . . . He sanctified Himself that we might be sanctified. Christ is made unto us redemption . . . everything that Adam lost, Jesus redeemed at the tremendous price of His precious blood. Through His blood we have redemption, the forgiveness of sins . . . and without the shedding of blood there is no remission. The blood of Jesus Christ, God's Son, cleanseth us from all sin! Let me repeat for emphasis: The most precious, priceless thing known to God or man is salvation.

Yes, this **salvation is great in its cost.**

The only possible way poor, miserable, wretched, despicable sinners could have been transformed into heirs of God, joint-heirs with Christ (we are sons of God) is through God's great love. We were, in times past, children of wrath. We walked according to this world, according to the prince of the power of the air who is the devil. We had our conversation, in times past, in the lust of our flesh. We fulfilled the desires of the mind and of the flesh, and we were by nature the children of wrath. "BUT GOD, WHO IS RICH IN MERCY, FOR HIS GREAT LOVE WHEREWITH HE LOVED US, even when we were dead in sins, hath quickened us together with Christ, (by grace ye are saved)" (Eph. 2:4-5). We have salvation because God loved us with a "GREAT LOVE." God's love is a fathomless ocean; a mine of wealth. His love is a lasting spring, an artesian well, a glorious provision, a sun of warmth, a gigantic lifting power. His love is an unceasing inspiration! No wonder the Holy Ghost refers to the love that saved us as "GREAT LOVE."

Those of us who are saved are saved with a "great salvation." Great because God is its source. Great because we are salvation's object . . . enemies of God when God provided this great salvation. Christ IS this salvation. Deliverance from sin, the devil and hell is the **meaning** of our great salvation. It is powerful to deliver us from the world, the flesh, and the devil. Faith receives this great salvation . . . holiness in Christ is the result, and glory in Heaven with Jesus is its consummation. Yes, our salvation is truly GREAT.

Those of us who possess this great salvation are thrilled with great joy that is unspeakable and full of glory. In the book of Acts, Philip went down to Samaria and preached the Gospel of the Lord Jesus Christ. Many were born again, brought into the knowledge of this great salvation, and the Bible tells us, "There WAS GREAT JOY IN THAT CITY" (Acts 8:8).

When the angel announced the birth of Jesus, he said, "Fear not: for, behold, I bring you good tidings OF GREAT JOY, which shall be to all people" (Luke 2:10). The Saviour is the secret of the joy of this great salvation. He is not only the secret — He is the substance of it. He is the supply. He

126

is the source. He is this "great salvation." HIS joy makes our joy full and lasting. I especially love the way Peter expresses the joy of our salvation: "Whom having not seen, ye love; in whom, though now ye see Him not, yet believing, ye rejoice WITH JOY UNSPEAKABLE AND FULL OF GLORY" (I Peter 1:8).

Those of us who possess this great salvation are strengthened with great power: "And with GREAT POWER gave the apostles witness of the resurrection of the Lord Jesus: and great grace was upon them all" (Acts 4:33). From any angle you may look at this great salvation, from whatever aspect we look or study this great salvation, we find great, **great,** GREAT! Thank God we have great strength in our great salvation!

Our great salvation **brings to our heart great peace.** "Great peace have they which love thy law: and nothing shall offend them" (Psalm 119:165). To love God's holy word is to find the joy of His great grace and salvation . . . the tenderness of His love, the holiness of Himself, and the peace that passeth all understanding. To the disciples, Jesus said "Peace I leave with you, my peace I give unto you: not as the world giveth, give I unto you. Let not your heart be troubled, neither let it be afraid" (John 14:27). This **great salvation** brings great PEACE to our hearts.

One of these glorious days when Jesus comes to the world, His saints will come with Him. He will come first in the Rapture FOR them, and then when He returns to the earth, we (the Bride) will return with Him. He will come in great glory. He will not have that glory apart from His saints . . . His Bride. It would be no glory to Him if we were not with Him, because He purchased us; He purchased the church with His own precious blood.

"And then shall they see the Son of man coming in a cloud with power and great glory" (Luke 21:27).

God's great mercy is so great that His mercy forgives great sins committed by great sinners over a great period of time; and then gives great favor and blessing, and great privileges to these great sinners who are recipients of His great mercy. He gives to us great pleasures in this life, and eternal enjoyment in the great Heaven of the Great God. We must receive His great mercy, or we will have no mercy whatsoever. The only kind of mercy, grace and love God knows, is GREAT; therefore, "How shall we escape if we neglect so great salvation!"

Let me say one more thing, "Whosoever shall call upon the name of the Lord shall be saved." Let me say again, "They that come to Me, I will in no wise cast out." Hear these words, "Come unto me, all ye that labour and are heavy-laden and I will give you rest." These are precious too: "As many as received Him, to them gave He power to become the sons of God, even to them that believe on His name . . . which were born . . . born of God."

These words are not to be taken lightly: "Believe on the Lord Jesus Christ and thou shalt be saved." Yes, salvation has been brought down. Salvation is finished. Salvation is presented to you, dear reader, and the only way you or I or any other person will ever be saved is to simply receive the finished work of the Lord Jesus by faith . . . trust Him, believe on Him, and HE does the saving! How shall we escape if we neglect salvation that cost so much and has been made so plain?

2. **Our salvation is great in its scope.**

"For God so loved THE WORLD, that He gave His only begotten Son, that whosoever believeth in Him should not perish, but have everlasting life" (John 3:16). This verse has been called the Gospel in a nutshell . . . and truly, it is. Two things I would like to point out here:

A. God loved the world . . . the whole world, all the world . . . every human being who has ever set foot on this earth. God loved ALL.

B. "Whosoever believeth" on Jesus shall be saved . . . shall have everlasting life. John 3:16 does not teach that a select, elect, predestined group can be saved, and all others must be damned. John 3:16 teaches clearly that God loved the world, Jesus died for the world, and **whosoever will** can be saved.

There are those in our land (around the world, for that matter) who teach that only a selected group known as "the elect" will be saved. I believe in the sovereignty of God. God knows who WILL be saved and who will NOT be saved. God is omnipotent, omniscient, and omnipresent; but the fact that God is sovereign does not determine whether I spend eternity in Heaven or in hell.

"He that believeth on Him is not condemned: but he that believeth not is condemned already, because he hath not believed in the name of the only begotten Son of God" (John 3:18). In that verse we are clearly taught that believers are free from condemnation. Unbelievers are condemned. The reason? Because they believe not on the name of the Son of God.

If the doctrine of hyper-Calvinism is true, then why did not the Holy Spirit clearly say "He that believeth not is condemned already because he was not elected"? It is left up to the individual whether to believe or to refuse to believe on the Lord Jesus Christ unto salvation. The SCOPE of our great salvation takes in everyone, excludes no one. Regardless of your nationality, the color of your skin, your social standing, your political standing, your monetary standing . . . "whosoever will" can be saved.

"The Lord is not slack concerning His promise, as some men count slackness; but is longsuffering to us-ward, not willing that any should perish, but that all should come to repentance" (II Peter 3:9).

The Lord is not willing that any should perish, but that all **(everyone)** should come to repentance. God has no joy in the death of the wicked. Let me say without apology and without reservation, If you are reading these lines, and die in your sins and wake up in hell fire, it will not be because you were not "elected" or "predestined" or "chosen;" it will not be the will of God. It will be because of your own stubborn will and your refusal to believe on the Lord Jesus Christ as your personal Saviour.

When Jesus came to this earth, the earth was filled with "religion," the scribes and the Pharisees, the elders and the chief priests . . . and of course at that particular time God was dealing with a specific nation — Israel. The Gentiles and all others were "dogs" in the eyes of the Israelites . . . they were outcasts, aliens without hope and strangers to the covenant of promise. How refreshing it must have been to the ears of the poor lepers, the downcast, the outcast, when Jesus said, "Come unto me, ALL YE THAT LABOUR AND ARE HEAVY LADEN, and I will give you rest!" (Matt. 11:28).

If the doctrine of hyper-Calvinism is true, if there are chosen ones who can be saved and all others must be damned, then why did not Jesus say, "Come unto me, all the elect, and I will give you rest"? Why did He not invite "Come unto me, all the chosen — and I will give you rest"? Why did He not say ,"Come unto me, all ye predestined — and I will give you rest"? You know why He did not say that? Jesus came into the world to save "whosoever" from "whatsoever" sin was damning them. Jesus came to save the Jew, the Gentile, the rich, the poor, the bond, the free . . . the down and out, the up and out . . . **"whosoever"** was His invitation. ALL are invited to "Come," and "whosoever comes" can be saved.

The apostle Paul sheds light on who can be saved: "That if thou shalt confess with thy mouth the Lord Jesus, and shalt believe in thine heart that God hath raised Him from the dead, thou shalt be saved. For with the heart man believeth unto righteousness; and with the mouth confession is made unto salvation. For the scripture saith, Whosoever believeth on Him shall not be ashamed. For there is no difference between the Jew and the Greek: for the same Lord over all is rich unto all that call upon Him. FOR WHOSOEVER SHALL CALL UPON THE NAME OF THE LORD SHALL BE SAVED" (Romans 10:9-13).

Paul declares, "The scriptures saith, Whosoever believeth on Him shall not be ashamed. For there is no difference between the Jew and the Greek: for the same Lord over all is rich unto all that call upon Him." Paul then invites, "Whosoever shall call upon the name of the Lord shall be saved!" Thank God, the invitation is to all . . . ALL are included, NOT ONE is excluded. The invitation is to ALL.

Listen to the last invitation to sinners, given in the Bible: "And the Spirit and the bride say, Come. And let him that heareth say, Come. And let him that is athirst come. AND WHOSOEVER WILL, LET HIM TAKE THE WATER OF LIFE FREELY" (Rev. 22:17). The Holy Spirit invites ALL to come. The church (the Bride) invites ALL to come. The invitation is to the thirsty. Why did not the Spirit of God say "Let him that is elected, come." Or "Let him that is chosen, come." Simply because the invitation is to "Whosoever is thirsty!" If you are hungry and thirsty for God, you are invited to come, regardless of who you are, regardless of what you have done. If you are thirsty for God and for salvation, come to the Lord Jesus and HE will satisfy your thirst. "Whosoever will, let him drink of the water of life freely!"

God created man in His own image (Gen. 1:26-27). God breathed into his nostrils the breath of life and man became a living soul. God put Adam in the Garden of Eden. God gave Adam instructions. Adam, of his own free will, chose to believe and follow his wife's invitation, instead of obeying God's command; therefore, Adam fell into sin and death;

131

and through the disobedience of one man, sin and death moved upon all men. But thank God, God so loved man and the whole wide world, that He gave His only begotten Son that **whosoever** — ANY man desiring to be saved — could be saved.

"Wherefore as by one man sin entered into the world, and death by sin; and so death passed upon all men, for that all have sinned: For until the law sin was in the world: but sin is not imputed when there is no law. Nevertheless death reigned from Adam to Moses, even over them that had not sinned after the similitude of Adam's transgression, who is the figure of Him that was to come. But not as the offence, so also is the free gift. For if through the offence of one many be dead, much more the grace of God, and the gift by grace, which is by one man, Jesus Christ, hath abounded unto many. And not as it was by one that sinned, so is the gift: for the judgment was by one to condemnation, but the free gift is of many offences unto justification. For if by one man's offence death reigned by one; much more they which receive abundance of grace and of the gift of righteousness shall reign in life by one, Jesus Christ. Therefore as by the offence of one judgment came upon all men to condemnation; even so by the righteousness of one the free gift came upon all men unto justification of life. For as by one man's disobedience many were made sinners, so by the obedience of one shall many be made righteous. Moreover the law entered, that the offence might abound. But where sin abounded, grace did much more abound; that as sin hath reigned unto death, even so might grace reign through righteousness unto eternal life by Jesus Christ our Lord" (Rom. 5:12-21).

Please read verse 18 very carefully — and believe it: "Therefore as by the offence of one judgment came upon ALL men to condemnation, even so by the righteousness of one the free gift CAME UPON ALL MEN into justification of life."

Through the sin of Adam, all died spiritually. We are born in sin, shapen in iniquity. But hallelujah! Through the obedience of the second Adam ALL can be saved . . . all who desire to be saved and all who come to God by Christ Jesus.

There is a verse in the Old Testament that will stop every mouth that preaches that some are selected, elected, and chosen while others must be damned. "ALL we like sheep have gone astray; we have turned every one to his own way; and the Lord hath laid on Him the iniquity of us ALL" (Isa. 53:6). Notice carefully: ALL mankind went astray. ALL have sinned and come short of the glory of God. There is NONE righteous, no, not one! We have ALL gone out of the way . . . but Jehovah God laid on Jesus the **iniquity of us all.** Jesus paid the penalty for every sin that has been committed by every man, including Adam through the last man who will live on this earth in a natural body. Jesus shed enough blood to cover every sin that ever has been committed, that is being committed, that ever WILL be committed. Jesus died for the sins of the whole wide world — and "whosoever will" may drink freely of the water of life and be saved by the marvelous grace of God, and have their name written in the Lamb's book of Life.

John tells us in these precious words, "My little children, these things write I unto you, that ye sin not. And if any man sin, we have an advocate with the Father, Jesus Christ the righteous; AND HE IS THE PROPITIATION FOR OUR SINS: AND NOT FOR OURS ONLY, BUT ALSO FOR THE SINS OF THE WHOLE WORLD" (I John 2:1-2).

Jesus died according to the Scriptures. He was buried and He rose again according to the scriptures. And "He that heareth my word, believeth on Him that sent me, hath everlasting life and shall not come into condemnation but is passed from death unto life." That is God's holy Word, and it cannot be changed or altered in spite of the hyper-Calvinists and those who teach that only a select, elect chosen group will be saved.

Let me assure you again that I believe in the Sovereignty of God; but I also believe in the free will of man. God made man a free moral agent. God has given man the opportunity to choose — and your eternal destiny depends upon whether you receive or reject the Lord Jesus Christ. Receive Him — and live! But if you reject Him you will spend eternity in the lake of fire that burns with brimstone . . . not because it is God's will, not because you were not elected to be saved . . . but if you burn in hell you will do so because of your own stubborn will . . . because you chose to serve self and sin and lust instead of receiving the Lord Jesus Christ." Believe on the Lord Jesus Christ and thou shalt be saved . . . and thy house" (Acts 16:31).

"How shall we escape if we neglect so great salvation?" Great — First in its cost. Great — Second in its scope.

3. This glorious salvation which we possess in Christ Jesus **is great in its climax.**

"For if we believe that Jesus died and rose again, even so them also which sleep in Jesus will God bring with Him. For this we say unto you by the word of the Lord, that we which are alive and remain unto the coming of the Lord shall not prevent them which are asleep. For the Lord Himself shall descend from Heaven with a shout, with the voice of the archangel, and with the trump of God: and the dead in Christ shall rise first: Then we which are alive and remain shall be caught up together with them in the clouds, to meet the Lord in the air: and so shall we ever be with the Lord. WHEREFORE COMFORT ONE ANOTHER WITH THESE WORDS" (I Thess. 4:14-18).

This salvation that we have in the Lord Jesus Christ saves us from the penalty of sin. The wages of sin is death. The penalty of sin is death. When sin is finished it brings forth death. Death and sin are synonymous. But when we are saved we are delivered from the power of death. We are raised from spiritual deadness: "And you hath He quickened (made alive) who were dead in trespasses and in sins" (Eph. 2:1). Paul declares, "She that liveth in pleasure is dead while she lives." Sin and death are synonymous, but when we are born again we are alive in Christ, with a life that is everlasting. We live forever because HE lives forever. We have eternal life because "from everlasting to everlasting, thou art God!" (Psalm 90:1-2).

This salvation saves us from the penalty of sin — but that is not all. This great salvation saves us from the power of sin. "We are more than conquerors through Him that loved us" (Rom. 8:31-39). Read those verses carefully. Then, we do overcome the world because greater is the God in us than the god of this world — who of course is the devil (I John 4:4). We conquer because God lives in us.

"Whosoever is born of God overcometh the world: and this is the victory that overcometh the world, even our faith" (I John 5:4). This great salvation saves us from the penalty of sin and daily saves us from the power of sin. And then, at the end of life's journey this great salvation will save us from the very presence of sin. If we live until the rapture of the church, we believers will be caught up to meet Jesus in the clouds in the air; but if we should depart this life before the Rapture, if Jesus delays His coming and we depart this life, "To be absent from the body is to be present with the Lord." Please read II Corinthians 5:1-8. When a believer dies, he goes immediately to be with the Lord Jesus.

"For to me to live is Christ, TO DIE IS GAIN; but if I live in the flesh this is the fruit of my labour: yet what I shall choose I wot not. For I am in a strait betwixt two, having a desire to depart, and to be with Christ; which is far better: nevertheless to abide in the flesh is more needful for you" (Phil. 1:21-24). Paul testified, "To die is gain." Paul said, "I desire to leave this world and to be with Christ which would be far better." The salvation we have does not stop or cease at the grave. When we depart this life, we go immediately to be with the Lord Jesus in Paradise.

The rich man died and opened his eyes in hell. The beggar Lazarus died and was carried by the angels into Abraham's bosom . . . the place of rest, the Paradise of the righteous. Thank God for so great salvation!

Not only will this salvation take us to Paradise into the presence of the Lord Jesus Christ, but hear these precious words: "Behold what manner of love the Father hath bestowed upon us, that we should be called the sons of God: therefore the world knoweth us not, because it knew Him not. Beloved, now are we the sons of God, and it doth not yet appear what we shall be: but we know that when He shall appear, we shall be like Him; for we shall see Him as He is" (I John 3:1-2).

This great salvation provides redemption for the spirit and a body just like the Lord's glorious body for the world to come. We will have a body that will never be sick, never hurt, never die. We will be like Him, we will see Him as He is. I am looking forward to that grand and glorious day when I will have a body untouched by sin . . . a glorified body, a glorious body like unto His resurrection body.

I am so happy that I can say with David, "The Lord is my Shepherd, I shall not want. He maketh me to lie down in green pastures, He leadeth me beside the still waters, He restoreth my soul. He leadeth me in the paths of righteousness for His name's sake. YEA, THOUGH I WALK THROUGH THE VALLEY OF THE SHADOW OF DEATH I WILL FEAR NO EVIL, FOR THOU ART WITH ME. THY ROD AND THY STAFF THEY COMFORT ME. Thou preparest a table before me in the presence of mine enemies: thou anointest my head with oil; my cup runneth over. Surely goodness and mercy shall follow me all the days of my life: AND I WILL DWELL IN THE HOUSE OF THE

LORD FOREVER" (Psalm 23). Hallelujah! I can say with David, "The Lord is my Shepherd." And if I DO walk through the valley of the shadow of death, I will not be afraid, for Jesus will be with me. He will hold my hand . . . thank God, what a great provision in a great salvation!

I know that goodness and mercy will follow me every day that I live on this earth. Then when I depart this life I will dwell in the house of God forever, because "In my Father's house are many mansions." Jesus said He would go to prepare a place for me, and He said He would come again and receive me unto Himself, and I am looking forward to that glorious day (John 14:1-6).

In closing let me give you a precious, precious promise: "And I heard a voice from Heaven saying unto me, Write, Blessed are the dead which die in the Lord from henceforth: Yea, saith the Spirit, that they may rest from their labours; and their works do follow them" (Rev. 14:13).

I know I am saved. I am happy in the Lord. I enjoy my salvation. I get a great thrill out of living for Jesus and trying to win others to the Lamb of God. I am glad that my redemption was finished on Calvary. I am redeemed by and through His precious blood. But I am glad that my salvation did not stop with redemption. I am glad He gives me the grace, the courage and the power to LIVE for Him daily. I am glad He will not permit me to be tempted above that which I am able to bear, but that He will with the temptation make a way for me to escape (I Cor. 10:13). Read it, memorize it, believe it, live by it and die by it.

I am glad that at the end of life's journey I will either go to be with Jesus in the rapture, or if He delays His coming the climax of my salvation will not be at the grave because Jesus will go with me through the valley of the shadow, and He will go with me all the way to the Paradise of God . . . and I will still be happy because the Bible tells me "Blessed are the dead which die in the Lord . . . happy are the dead which die in the Lord!"

This great salvation brings great joy to my heart because I am redeemed. This great salvation brings great joy to my heart because I know He is able to keep that which I have committed unto Him against that day. This great salvation brings great joy to my heart because I know at the end of life's journey Jesus will be waiting . . . He will go with me, He will give me a resting place in Paradise. And then in the sweet bye and bye He will give me a body just like His own glorious body and I will dwell with Him in that celestial city John saw coming down from God out of Heaven, adorned as a bride for her husband.

Do you know this great salvation? If you do not, please bow your head, close your eyes and receive the Lord Jesus right now! "As many as received Him, to them gave He the power to become the sons of God, even them that believe on His name, which were born . . . born of God." (John 1:12-13). Bow your head, receive the Lord Jesus, accept this great salvation and then you too will be blessed . . . you too can say, "Blessed assurance, Jesus is Mine! Oh, what a foretaste of glory divine!"

May God bless you richly if you are born again, and may God save you, my dear reader, if you are not saved.

The Tomb of Time

THE TOMB OF TIME

The devil has never asked any person to sign a contract to go to hell. He has never asked anyone to promise him never to be converted and become a child of God. All Satan asks of any person is one day at a time. In other words, if you read this sermon, and at the close of your reading he can persuade you to ignore the message and do nothing about your eternal welfare, he will be satisfied. He does not ask you to promise that you will never read another sermon, or that you will never go to church again. He just wants you to reject Jesus NOW; refuse to be saved TODAY and if he can cause you, today, to put off salvation until some other time—or as Felix said, until **"a more convenient season,"** he knows there are ten thousand ways by which you can die and go to hell in the next twenty-four hours! So — his program for you is to get you to put off until tomorrow what you should do today — even this very moment: "Behold, NOW is the accepted time; behold, NOW is the day of salvation" (II Cor. 6: 2 b).

The following Scriptures will serve as a foundation for this message on the "tomb of time":

James 4:12-17: "There is one lawgiver, who is able to save and to destroy: who art thou that judgest another? Go to now, ye that say, To day or to morrow we will go into such a city, and continue there a year, and buy and sell, and get gain: Whereas ye know not what shall be on the morrow. For what is your life? It is even a vapour, that appeareth for a little time, and then vanisheth away. For that ye ought to say, If the Lord will, we shall live, and do this, or that. But now ye rejoice in your boastings: all such rejoicing is evil. Therefore to him that knoweth to

141

do good, and doeth it not, to him it is sin."

Proverbs 27:1: "Boast not thyself of to morrow; for thou knowest not what a day may bring forth."

Exodus 8:10 and 15: "And (Pharoah) said, To morrow .... But when Pharoah saw that there was respite, he hardened his heart, and hearkened not unto them; as the Lord had said."

In these Scriptures the Holy Spirit points out to us the danger in saying, **"Tomorrow!"** James warns us not to say we will go to this city or that city, and remain there for a certain length of time, and buy, sell, and get gain, because we do not know what shall be on tomorrow. What IS life? Life is like a vapor — it appears, and then it quickly vanishes. Life is so short and death is so sure, we ought to say, **"If it is the Lord's will,** we shall live and do this or that." Our very existence depends upon God's will, and if it is NOT His will, we shall not even **live.**

According to the Scriptures, we should not make any move or plan without seeking God's will in the matter. We have no right to boast about tomorrow, because the tomorrows are not ours. We possess today — this moment; but tomorrow, for us, may never come.

Pharoah is a good example of the danger in procrastination. If you have studied the book of Exodus, you will recall how God told Moses to go to Pharoah and tell him to let the children of Israel go. Moses went to Pharoah and delivered God's message — but Pharoah said, **"Tomorrow!"** Again and again he promised, "Tomorrow." You know the sad story: Pharoah's "tomorrow" never came. He was drowned, along with his armies, and he went to hell from the bottom of the Red Sea!

Dear friend, take warning: **"Tomorrow" is the mortuary, the funeral parlor, of hell.** There are many things we can count on, but we cannot count on tomorrow. The days that are behind us will never return. **Today is ours** — moment by moment. What we have done in the past has forever entered into the tomb of time. Yesterday is dissolved in the eternity behind us as a drop of water is lost in the vastness of the ocean. Our yesterdays are gone and the tomorrows are not ours. **This moment** is ours, and we should seriously consider our eternal destiny. This moment ask yourself the eternal question, "Are my sins covered by the blood of Jesus? Am I born again?" And if you are not, do not say "Next Sunday I will be saved... The next revival at our church I will give my heart to Christ." If you put off salvation until next Sunday or the next revival — or even until the next hour — you may spend eternity in hell! **May** God help you right now, this moment, to receive the Lord Jesus Christ. In the language of Isaiah, "Seek ye the Lord while He may be found. Call upon Him while He is near" (Isa. 55:6).

In discussing our subject for this message, I want us to consider several passages of Scripture. We will begin with several verses from Zechariah:

"In the eighth month, in the second year of Darius, came the word of the Lord unto Zechariah, the son of Berechiah, the son of Iddo the prophet, saying, The Lord hath been sore displeased with your fathers. Therefore say thou unto them, Thus saith the Lord of hosts: Turn ye unto me, saith the Lord of hosts, and I will turn unto you, saith the Lord of hosts. Be ye not as your fathers, unto whom the former prophets have cried, saying, Thus saith the Lord of hosts; Turn ye now from your evil ways, and from your evil doings: **but they did not hear, nor hearken unto me, saith the Lord.** Your fathers, **where are they?** And the prophets, do they live for ever? But my words and my statutes, which I commanded my servants the prophets, did they not take hold of your fathers? and they returned

143

and said, Like as the Lord of hosts thought to do unto us, according to our ways, and according to our doings, so hath He dealt with us" (Zech. 1:1-6).

Zechariah was a prophet of God with a message to the remnant of God's chosen people who returned to their own land after the seventy years of Babylonian captivity. Certainly all that we need do to see how God feels about sin and rebellion in the life of His people is to read the history of the nation Israel. When they followed Jehovah God and worshipped Him AS God, heaven's best was theirs; but when they rebelled against Him and turned to idols, God dealt severely with them even though they were His chosen people. If God spared not "the natural branches," woe be unto us who are not of the elect, the covenant nation of Israel.

I know that in this day of grace God saves Jew and Gentile alike; but if He dealt severely with HIS people Israel, then how can WE hope to escape if we neglect so great salvation in this marvelous day of God's grace?

Zechariah thundered out in terms easily understood that these people of the remnant were to turn to God from evil, and follow Him. If they did as their fathers had done, they too would be cut off; but what I would point out in this message is the warning, **"Turn ye NOW!"** God deals in the eternal present; He does not deal in yesterdays nor in tomorrows. Turn NOW — not tomorrow, not next week, not next Sunday, not during the next revival — **but turn to Him now.** If you refuse to turn to Him now, **tomorrow may be eternally too late for you!**

Isaiah 1:18-20 says, "Come now, and let us reason together, saith the Lord: though your sins be as scarlet, they shall be as white as snow; though they be red like crimson, they shall be as wool. If ye be willing and obedient, ye shall eat the good of the land: But if ye refuse and rebel, ye shall be devoured with the sword: for the mouth of the Lord hath spoken it." (I trust you will take your Bible in hand and read the first 17 verses of this chapter.)

In these verses, Isaiah solemnly warned Israel, and then he gave them God's invitation: "Come NOW, and let us reason together, saith the Lord." But the people did not obey. They refused to come to God and permit Him to reason with them. We find their answer in Isaiah 30:15-17:

"For thus saith the Lord God, the Holy One of Israel; In returning and rest shall ye be saved; in quietness and in confidence shall be your strength: **and ye would not.** But ye said, No; for we will flee upon horses; therefore shall ye flee: and, We will ride upon the swift; therefore shall they that pursue you be swift. One thousand shall flee at thy rebuke of one; at the rebuke of five shall ye flee: till ye be left as a beacon upon the top of a mountain, and as an ensign on an hill."

In these verses, God offered to save His people if they would return — but they would not! They said, "No! We will flee from our enemies on swift horses." God reminded them that the horses of their enemies could also be swift.

Paul said, "If God be for us, who can be against us?" (Rom. 8:31). But by the same token, **if God be against us, we cannot hope to win.** God and you comprise a majority over any crowd; but without God (regardless of the crowd), you are outnumbered. You cannot win without God; but in Him, through Him, and with Him YOU CANNOT LOSE!

Through the prophet Isaiah God invited Israel to come and reason together with Him — but they refused, and rebelled against Him. In Isaiah 1:19 we read, **"If ye be willing and obedient, ye shall eat the good of the land; but if ye refuse and rebel, ye shall be devoured with the sword: for the mouth of the Lord hath spoken it."**

All we need do is turn to the history of Israel, read that

history as it is laid down in the Word of God, and clearly see that **they were devoured by the sword.** I suppose no people on earth have ever suffered such a deluge of blood as Israel has suffered, and in many places they are still being severely persecuted today. They asked for it — and they are still receiving the rod of judgment.

But again — the primary thought I would impress upon you who read this message is the fact that **God deals in the eternal present**: "Come NOW and let us reason together, saith the Lord." If you are not saved, if you are not a child of God, He wants to reason with you NOW, this very moment — not when you finish reading this sermon, not next Sunday when you go to church, not when you attend the next revival meeting, not when you decide you want to be saved. God wants to reason with you NOW; and if you refuse to hear His voice, if you refuse to yield to the wooing of His Spirit now, **five minutes from now** you may find yourself in eternity, hopelessly lost without God!

I could write pages upon pages about experiences I have had through the years of my evangelistic ministry across this country and around the world; I could tell of many who have gone out to meet God only minutes after leaving the services where I preached the Word of God. I have had the heartbreaking experience of having two men drop dead before me as I talked with them about their soul. I could tell of others who have been in the services, rejected God's invitation and started to their homes, never to reach them. Time and space will not permit me to give you all of these instances, but let me warn you that "Today is the day of salvation, NOW is the accepted time."

This is the moment Jesus stands ready and anxious to save you, and if you rebel and refuse His glorious salvation you will reap the judgment of Almighty God. If you hear

His voice, harden not your heart. If the still small voice of the Spirit of God is calling you right now, I beg you to surrender to Jesus this very moment. Do not put it off even until you finish reading this sermon. Bow your head and invite the Lord Jesus to come into your heart right now — and He WILL! He promised, and He will keep His promise, for God cannot lie (Heb. 6:18; Tit. 1:2).

Our next passage of Scripture comes from Luke 14:16-18: "Then said He unto him, a certain man made a great supper, and bade many: and sent his servant at supper time to say to them that were bidden, **Come; for all things are now ready. And they all with one consent began to make excuse.**"

We find the same account given in different words in Matthew 22:1-8: "And Jesus answered and spake unto them again by parables, and said, The kingdom of heaven is like unto a certain king, which made a marriage for his son, and sent forth his servants to call them that were bidden to the wedding: and they would not come. Again, he sent forth other servants, saying, Tell them that are bidden, Behold, I have prepared my dinner; my oxen and my fatlings are killed, and all things are ready: come unto the marriage. But they made light of it, and went their ways, one to his farm, another to his merchandise: and the remnant took his servants, and entreated them spitefully, and slew them. But when the king heard thereof, he was wroth; and he sent forth his armies, and destroyed those murderers, and burned up their city. Then saith he to his servants, The wedding is ready..."

Everything that might have been needed or required to attend a wedding in that day was furnished by the king. Those who were invited were simply asked to bring themselves. The invitation was, **"Come, for all things are now ready!"** This is a picture of salvation. The King of

147

kings and Lord of lords has provided everything we need. Before Jesus bowed His head on His pulseless breast and gave up the Ghost, He said, "It is finished!" (John 19:30); and by that declaration He was announcing to the heavenly Father and to the whole wide world that every detail of redemption had been taken care of. The ransom had been paid in full, and salvation in every detail had been completed. "For in Him dwelleth all the fulness of the Godhead bodily. **And ye are complete in Him,** which is the head of all principality and power" (Col. 2:9, 10).

I have been preaching the Gospel for many years, and the hardest thing on earth for me to get people to accept is the fact that salvation is **finished;** it is **complete,** and it is ours simply for the asking. Not one thing can we add to God's finished salvation, for **Jesus paid it all.** He satisfied the heart of God, and there is nothing WE can do to satisfy God except believe on His Son and accept His finished work. The only way you or I will ever stand before God in peace is to stand there with His Son, the Lord Jesus.

In Matthew 10:32, 33 Jesus said, "Whosoever therefore shall confess me before men, him will I confess also before my Father which is in heaven. But whosoever shall deny me before men, him will I also deny before my Father which is in heaven." There is but one Mediator between God and men — the man Christ Jesus (I Tim. 2:5). We must trust fully in Jesus if we hope to stand before God and hear Him say, "Enter thou the joys of thy Lord."

The king's invitation not only announced that all things were ready, but the people were invited to come NOW. The supper was ready, the fatlings were killed, the lambs were prepared, the food was on the table. Those who were invited were reminded that it was time to eat. "Come, for all things are NOW ready!"

I intentionally repeat in order to drive this solemn fact

148

deep into your mind: The tomorrows are not yours, the yesterdays are swallowed up in the eternity behind you. **The eternal present** is the time in which God deals with sinners and saves souls. Dear friend, if you are NOT saved, all things are ready NOW and if you reject the invitation of the Lord Jesus now, before tomorrow your body may be in the mortuary; ten minutes from now your soul may be in hell. **Today** is the day, **now** is the time. Tomorrow may be everlastingly, eternally too late!

In Matthew 22:7 we are told that "when the king heard thereof, he was wroth: **and he sent forth his armies, and destroyed those murderers, and burned up their city.**" Sin and destruction are synonymous. "The wages of sin is death... When sin is finished it bringeth forth death." If you follow sin (and yet escape its damnation), you will be the first human being ever to ignore God, serve the devil — and get away with it! Sin brings judgment. You cannot ignore God, refuse His salvation, and get by with it. He is inviting you to the marriage supper in the sky; but if you hope to attend that glorious gathering, you must be saved — and the time is NOW.

I am aware that the following Scripture points directly to the door of the Laodicean church; but it can also be applied to the human heart, without damaging or warping the Scriptures: "Behold, I stand at the door, and knock: if any man hear my voice, and open the door, I will come in to him, and will sup with him, and he with me" (Rev. 3:20). If Jesus is standing at your heart's door, knocking, I advise you to open the door and let Him in; for if He departs, He may never return.

"Boast not thyself of tomorrow, for thou knowest not what a day may bring forth ... Seek ye the Lord while He may be found; call on Him while He is near ... If you hear His voice, harden not your heart." Is Jesus knocking at your heart's door? If you hear the still small voice of the Holy Spirit asking entrance into your heart, by faith throw open the door this very moment and invite Jesus to come in. He will — and you will know it; and until your dying day you will thank God for the very moment you put your trust in Him.

Before leaving this part of our message, let me assure you that "all things are now ready." All that you need, you will find in Jesus. Receive Him, believe on Him, accept His finished work — and God will write your name in the Lamb's book of life. Come NOW — and be saved!

If I could see, in one great audience, all the people who will read these lines, and I should ask the question, "How many of you plan to spend eternity in hell?" not one person would lift his hand and say, "Preacher Greene, I have MY mind made up to spend eternity in hell!" Not one person who reads this message plans to burn in hell.

If, in that one great audience, I should ask every born again child of God to lift his hand as a testimony to Jesus, I am sure there would be many who could not raise their hands as a testimony that they are born again. ALL RIGHT: If you are reading these lines and you do not plan to spend eternity in hell, let me ask you a very timely question: **When DO you plan to be saved?** At just what time in your life DO you plan to put your trust and faith in the Lord Jesus Christ as your personal Saviour?

There are varied and sundry answers given to that question, but I can assure you that every answer that puts off salvation until a later, more convenient season, **is of the devil.** I said in the outset of this message that the devil has never asked any sinner to sign a contract to go to hell, or to promise never to be converted. He is too smart for that; he is a wise deceiver. He has had 6,000 years' experience in damning souls and he is no fool. He knows bet-

150

ter than to ask you to promise that you will **never** be saved, that you will burn in hell. He simply suggests to you that you **put off** salvation until tomorrow, or next Sunday, or perhaps until Easter — or even when you get married and settle down. In many (and subtle) ways the devil suggests that you postpone salvation until a more convenient time — or until you have straightened up some things you feel must be taken care of, or until you feel that you are capable of living the kind of life a Christian should live. If your mind is harboring any such suggestions, I assure you on the basis of God's Word that those suggestions are of the devil.

Jesus says, "Come NOW — and let us reason together! Come NOW — for all things are now ready. Receive me, believe on me, call on my name and do it NOW; because now is the accepted time, and today (not tomorrow) is the day of salvation." If the devil can get you to reject Jesus today, he knows there are ten thousand ways through which he can damn you tomorrow!

"Again, a new commandment I write unto you, which thing is true in Him and in you: because the darkness is past, and the true light now shineth" (I John 2:8). In this marvelous passage we learn that the darkness is forever behind us because the True Light has come into the world and made it possible for all who desire to know the way of life to be able to understand and find that Way.

"In the beginning was the Word, and the Word was with God, and the Word was God. The same was in the beginning with God. All things were made by Him; and without Him was not any thing made that was made. In Him was life; and the life was the light of men. And the light shineth in darkness; and the darkness comprehended it not. There was a man sent from God, whose name was John. The same came for a witness, to bear witness of the Light, that all men through him might believe. He was not that Light, but was sent to bear witness of that Light. That was the true Light, which lighteth every man that cometh into the world. He was in the world, and the world was made by Him, and the world knew Him not. He came unto His own, and His own received Him not. But as many as received Him, to them gave He power to become the sons of God, even to them that believe on His name: Which were born, not of blood, nor of the will of the flesh, nor of the will of man, but of God" (John 1:1-14).

The True Light of which John is speaking here (and also in his first Epistle) is none other than the Lord Jesus Christ, **the Light of the world.** There is absolutely no excuse for any sinner going on in sin, for the Light has come, sin has been shown up, unveiled, and the exceeding sinfulness of sin made known through the sufferings of Jesus on the cross. He came to pay sin's debt and ransom sinners from the devil. It took every heartache, every tear, every sorrow, every pain, all of the agony, the stripes on His back, the cruel mockings, the thorns on His brow, the spikes in His hands, the spear in His side, and every drop of blood He shed, to make our salvation possible! And all the forces of hell, all the powers of the underworld, cannot put out that Light.

Anyone wishing to know the Way of salvation can find that Way in the precious Word of God:

The Word is a lamp unto our feet and a light unto our path — Psalm 119:105.

The Word is the Power of God unto salvation — Romans 1:16.

The Word is a mirror — James 1:23-25.

The entrance of the Word giveth light — and the light of the Gospel brings salvation.

"He that believeth on Him is not condemned; but he

that believeth not is condemned already, because he hath not believed in the name of the only begotten Son of God. AND THIS IS THE CONDEMNATION, THAT LIGHT IS COME INTO THE WORLD, AND MEN LOVED DARKNESS RATHER THAN LIGHT, BECAUSE THEIR DEEDS WERE EVIL. For every one that doeth evil hateth the light, neither cometh to the light, lest his deeds should be reproved. But he that doeth truth cometh to the light, that his deeds may be made manifest, that they are wrought in God" (John 3:18-21).

In these verses we have enough Scripture to save the world if the world would only believe the truth contained therein. It is so very plain: Believers are not condemned. Those who do NOT believe are condemned **already** — and the **reason** they are condemned is because they refuse to believe on the name of the only begotten Son of God. Light has come into the world in the Person of the Lord Jesus Christ, and men are condemned because they refuse to come to that Light. If they would only come to Jesus, He would take away their condemnation. He would forgive their sin and the wrath of God would be removed from them. But sinners so often refuse to come to the Light because they know that the Light will reveal their wickedness and sin. To refuse to come to the Light is to bring the wrath of God down upon you. Jesus came into the world to seek and to save that which was lost and when men refuse to come to Jesus, God then has no choice but to mete out condemnation to them.

The Word of God tells us that Solomon was "wiser than all men" (I Kings 4:29-31). And in Proverbs 1:22-33 this great man of wisdom gives us this solemn warning: "How long, ye simple ones, will ye love simplicity? and the scorners delight in their scorning, and fools hate knowledge? Turn you at my reproof: behold, I will pour out my spirit unto you, I will make known my words unto you. Because I have called, and ye refused; I have stretched out my hand, and no man regarded; But ye have set at nought all my counsel, and would none of my reproof: I also will laugh at your calamity; I will mock when your fear cometh; When your fear cometh as desolation, and your destruction cometh as a whirlwind; when distress and anguish cometh upon you. Then shall they call upon me, but I will not answer; they shall seek me early, but they shall not find me: For that they hated knowledge, and did not choose the fear of the Lord: They would none of my counsel: They despised all my reproof. Therefore shall they eat of the fruit of their own way, and be filled with their own devices. For the turning away of the simple shall slay them, and the prosperity of fools shall destroy them. But whoso hearkeneth unto me shall dwell safely, and shall be quiet from fear of evil."

This passage of Scripture opens with a question: "How long . . . will the scorners delight in their scorning, and fools hate knowledge?" Then, through the pen of Solomon, Almighty God warns, "Turn you at my reproof! **I will pour out my Spirit upon you, I will make known my words unto you.**"

On the Day of Pentecost, God DID pour out the Holy Spirit, and in I John 2:27 we are told that the Holy Spirit will teach us ALL things. Therefore, any person who wants to be saved, can read the Word of God with an open mind and an open heart, and the Holy Spirit will convict and draw that person to the Lord Jesus Christ through the Word — the power of God unto salvation.

We are saved by God's grace, through faith. Saving faith comes by hearing, and hearing by the Word of God. The Holy Ghost is in the world to convict of sin, of righteousness, of judgment — and to draw men to God and "born" them into God's family.

Please read the following Scriptures: Ephesians 2:8, 9; Romans 10:17; John 16:7-9; 6:44; 3:5-7. The Spirit of God is the attending physician at the new birth. We are born of the Spirit when we exercise faith in God through the Lord Jesus Christ; but it is impossible for any sinner to be saved apart from hearing and believing the record God has given of His Son.

In our present passage from Proverbs, God warns: "I called — and you refused to hear my call. I stretched out my hand in mercy — but you refused it. I gave you counsel —but you set my counsel at nought. I reproved you — but you refused to accept my reproof. Therefore — I will laugh at your calamity and mock when your fear comes upon you!"

These people hated knowledge, and Proverbs 1:7 tells us that **"The fear of the Lord is the beginning of knowledge."** They did not fear God, they chose their own way; and they will therefore eat the **fruit** of their own way.

Dear reader, if you plunge into hell when you die, **it will not be by God's will that you go there!** It will be because of your own stubborn will, because you rejected Jesus Christ and refused His invitation. He calls, "Come **now** ... Though your sins be as scarlet, they shall be as white as snow. Come **now** ... and I will give you rest." That gracious invitation, rejected, will be the reason you spend eternity in hell.

I would remind you that Pharoah said, "Tomorrow ... tomorrow!" Time after time Moses delivered God's message to him; — each time he rejected that message, saying, **"Tomorrow,"** and his "tomorrow" cost him his eternal destiny with Jehovah God!

In Acts 24:24, 25 Paul reasoned with Felix: "And as he

155

reasoned of righteousness, temperance, and judgment to come, Felix trembled, and answered, **Go thy way for this time; when I have a convenient season, I will call for thee!**" So far as the record reveals, Felix never had another opportunity to be saved. He is in hell today, roasting in the flames of the damned when, had he heeded Paul's preaching of the Gospel and received Paul's Saviour, he would be rejoicing in the Paradise of God this moment. The devil saw to it that for Felix **"a more convenient season"** never came.

In the twenty-sixth chapter of Acts, Paul gives his mighty testimony before King Agrippa. Read the entire passage — time and space prohibit the giving of the entire text here. But read it — and weigh the words of the apostle as he witnessed before the king. As Paul was speaking, Festus said with a loud voice, "Paul, thou art beside thyself; much learning doth make thee mad!" Paul replied, "I am not mad, most noble Festus; but speak forth words of truth and soberness. For the king knoweth of these things, before whom also I speak freely: for I am persuaded that none of these things are hidden from him; for this thing was not done in a corner. **King Agrippa, believest thou the prophets?** I know that thou believest! Then Agrippa said unto Paul, ALMOST THOU PERSUADEST ME TO BE A CHRISTIAN" (Acts 26:24-28).

The mighty king Agrippa was almost persuaded to believe on the Lord Jesus Christ and receive Him as his personal Saviour — but **"almost** cannot avail, **almost** is but to fail. Sad, sad that bitter wail: **Almost — but lost!**" Agrippa is in hell today. Had he been **altogether persuaded** to become a Christian, if he had put his faith and trust in Jesus, he would be with Paul in Paradise, resting; but he postponed salvation— and that is all the devil asks any sinner to do! Just put off salvation until "tomorrow ... a more conveni-

156

ent season." Just be **"almost** persuaded," and Satan **knows** there are ten thousand ways he can damn your soul **before** you have another opportunity to be saved!